AUTISM, ANXIETY AND ME

AUTISM, ANXIETY AND ME

A Diary in Even Numbers

EMMA LOUISE BRIDGE

FOREWORD AND COMMENTARY BY PENELOPE BRIDGE

Jessica Kingsley *Publishers*
London and Philadelphia

First published in 2016
by Jessica Kingsley Publishers
73 Collier Street
London N1 9BE, UK
and
400 Market Street, Suite 400
Philadelphia, PA 19106, USA

www.jkp.com

Library of Congress Cataloging in Publication Data
Names: Bridge, Emma, author.
Title: Autism, anxiety and me : a diary in even numbers / Emma Bridge ;
foreword by Penelope Bridge.
Description: London ; Philadelphia : Jessica Kingsley Publishers, 2016.
Identifiers: LCCN 2016003681 | ISBN 9781785920776
Subjects: LCSH: Bridge, Emma. | Autistic people. | Autism spectrum disorders.
| Social anxiety.
Classification: LCC RC553.A88 B745 2016 | DDC 616.85/882--
dc23 LC record available at http://lccn.loc.gov/2016003681

British Library Cataloguing in Publication Data
A CIP catalogue record for this book is available from the British Library

ISBN 978 1 78592 077 6
eISBN 978 1 78450 336 9

Printed and bound in Great Britain

I would like to dedicate this book to
my family. I have a wonderful and
understanding immediate family. I also
have a rather large extended family who
have always been very supportive.
This book is also dedicated to my hamster
'Piggy/Moley'. I love to have her near me
when I write, stuffing her fat little cheeks
with food and providing a relaxing and
reassuring noise of gnawing and scrabbling.

CONTENTS

FOREWORD

My name is Penny Bridge and I am Emma's mum. I am a mother of three young adult children, a son and two girls with Asperger's syndrome, or autistic spectrum disorder (ASD) as it is more commonly called now. Although I have worked with children with special needs, including autism, within a primary school setting for a number of years and trained as an occupational therapist, my input in this book is based on our experience as a family and draws on what we have tried and found helpful to enable Emma and her siblings gain more independence and cope in what can be a very confusing and worrying world.

Emma told me she wanted to write this book to give an insight into her mind to anyone who was interested in autistic spectrum disorder and social anxiety. It is not a text book or a book designed to impart knowledge in an academic way. It is designed to give an honest and open insight into the thinking of her mind, her fears, her anxieties, her struggles to find what is 'normal' – 'Where do I fit in?' 'Why am I different?' It highlights issues that are faced by people, especially teenagers and young adults, on the autistic spectrum as they interact with the world and the people in it; as they struggle to be accepted and learn how to fit in, but also to be themselves.

The commentaries following each diary entry are not designed to be definitive or academic in nature; they are just thoughts and ideas as to how we have coped and dealt with issues as they have arisen, not only for Emma but for her sister too. Autism is a spectrum and everyone is an individual so these comments may not be helpful, but they may encourage or give ideas or just spark something in the reader's mind.

The book is easy to read, honest and open and will appeal to a wide audience – those who are living with someone with Asperger's syndrome/autistic spectrum disorder; those who want to understand a bit more how the autistic mind thinks from someone who should know; or those who think they may be on the spectrum or just feel different and for whom the book may trigger the thought 'that sounds like me'.

Penelope Bridge

INTRODUCTION

My name is Emma Louise Bridge. Most people just call me 'Emma' or 'Miss Bridge'. I always feel bad for my middle name because it rarely gets used.

Top Five Things About Me:

- I am short – 5ft 3" (three inches below average but not particularly small).

- I have strawberry blonde hair, which most people call 'ginger', although someone once called it 'spun gold'. I don't get how that is possible but it sounds nice.

- I have worn glasses since before my first birthday.

- I used to have braces but I don't now, although I still have an overbite.

- Currently my list of favourite things is: the Minions (including the two *Despicable Me* films), Disney, Horrible Histories, the Monarchy and Harry Potter. With secondary favourites being: Sharks, Marvel and History (Ancient–WWII), especially mythology. My favourite hobby is writing.

I had a hard time at school because of the first things on that list. Apparently, ginger hair with glasses and braces is a 'bully's dream'. I am not sure if that means they literally dream about that sort of thing because that would be weird. I have 'severe social anxiety' and 'autism'. If you look at my important file box, there is also a diagnosis for 'dyslexia, dyspraxia and visual processing issues', but that is not really that important for this book.

I have had autism since birth, although some people don't know this and assume I have only had it since I was diagnosed. I have had social anxiety since secondary school. It started as a result of bullying and then got worse with the death of a friend at 16 and then an incident at 19 that isn't appropriate for this book. I wanted to write this book because I love to write. The reason for the book is that my sister and I still struggle because of other people's lack of understanding of the condition. Plus I love to help people and hope that this book can broaden people's understanding but also offer advice that can be of use. I am sure I am not the only one who finds the world a scary and confusing place sometimes.

It has been really weird putting my diary in a form that can be read by people. Usually diaries are kept hidden – some even come with a lock and key – and not read by lots of people. Some even have 'keep out' written on them, and I saw one once with a skull and crossbones drawn on, presumably to be off-putting. However, some diaries have been published so I decided it would probably be okay. Plus I won't be there when you're reading it – wherever you like to read, I like to do it in the bath – and so it's not like I can know how you are going to react to what I have written.

I am 24 but sometimes I feel a lot younger. I think my brain has not yet caught up with my numerical age. Plus I look quite young, I have been told. People are always mistaking me for under 18. Someone said that when I am 30 I will love looking younger. Wonder if it happens the second I turn 30 or when I have been 30 for a bit. At least it should be helpful in making this book relatable for young teenagers all the way up to adults as it covers issues for all.

I hope what is written in this book is informative and fun to read. I haven't tried to make it fun on purpose because it was written as a diary and so I didn't know it was going to have an audience. However, people often laugh at things I say so I assume it is. Admittedly, people laugh when I say something I didn't intend as a joke. That happens rather a lot. I generally just let them laugh even though I don't get why it was funny.

Yours,
Emma Louise Bridge

HYPERSENSITIVITY AND GARDENING

Dear Diary,

I have done a survey of what is generally written to start these books and 'Dear Diary' won, with naming the diary something being a close second. I don't want to name something that cannot correct me if the name is wrong.

Anyway, I did some gardening today, for a relative who wanted some help with it. I was supposed to be 'dead-heading' flowers. It was actually very confusing, though. They don't tell you the right measurements to make them. I tried cutting them quite short to make sure I was covered, but then the plants looked pretty obliterated. So I tried cutting them a lot less and that was not enough – kind of looked like I was giving the plants a trim. I wish I had taken a ruler out with me and then I could have measured exactly halfway down the stem and at least that would have been even.

While I was contemplating whether I had time to go and get a ruler, the flies arrived. They aren't like regular flies. They are clearly flies that have body superiority complexes because they disguise themselves as wasps. I jumped back and escaped them. All I have to do is look at a bug and I feel like it's on me. I have been informed these flies can't hurt me, but that is beside the point. I just cannot stand the feeling of them touching me. I went back when it seemed they had left. However, nature apparently had a meeting and decided they didn't want me gardening today because a bee arrived. Now I like bees. They are cute and fat and they bumble between flowers looking very sweet. But I only like them from a reasonable distance. This bee invaded my personal space and landed on my leg. It then proceeded to try to walk up my leg. So I quite naturally panicked.

It is not that I am worried about being stung. It does hurt and I am a baby when it comes to pain so I wouldn't exactly like it. Seriously, paper cuts have been known to make me cry. I just really feel pain. Another wonderful side effect of being hypersensitive. But I am not allergic, so at least I know it won't kill me. No, the issue is the feeling of the insect on my skin. When one lands on me, it's like the rest of my body feels jealous and wants in on the party. Soon my entire body feels like it's got bees walking all over it. Numerous tiny little footsteps that itch and drive me crazy with the overwhelming feeling of being touched by something annoying everywhere. So I think it was perfectly reasonable I fled for the house and hid indoors. I have decided to give up on gardening. After all, this is why people pay professionals. People whose job it is to garden must have some kind of defence mechanism. Either that or they are not hypersensitive to touch.

Yours,
Emma Louise Bridge

P.S. Could not find out from my research how you are supposed to end these entries so just went for what seemed appropriate.

COMMENTARY

Emma's first diary entry shows up two issues that many autistic people face in life and which can cause difficulty and stress:

1. The first is an inability to complete a task given and a sense of failure because the task is not completed correctly, due to misunderstanding between the asker and the autistic person trying their best to do what they think they have been asked to do. With her literal mind, Emma followed the directions with the flowers exactly as given, with no interpretation. She first cut too much, then cut too little and ended up experiencing stress and not getting the job done.

To help with this issue the instructions should be made very clear in the first place, with no ambiguity about what is required. A demonstration of what is needed is always helpful. Generalised statements are not helpful. I find it necessary to be on hand to reassure and check progress, but without being patronising.

Another thing to bear in mind is not necessarily to expect a transfer of knowledge from one situation to another. New situations may need new explanations and learning.

2. The second issue is that of hypersensitivity. In this case Emma explains her hypersensitivity to touch, but autistic people may have hypersensitivity to many things, such as smell, taste, sound or visual stimuli. As one insect lands on her, she describes feeling as if she is covered in insects. This obviously affected her ability to enjoy the garden and complete the task she was trying to do.

One idea would be to use long-sleeved clothing to ensure the insects do not touch the skin, if this can be tolerated. Another idea would be to attempt tasks at different times of day when insects are less prevalent. Emma does not have a phobia of insects; it is hypersensitivity that causes the problem. This is important to distinguish, because a phobia needs to be treated differently; therapy with an outside agency specifically to address any particular phobia would be helpful.

A technique used to help with hypersensitivity is desensitisation which is taught by a trained therapist who can then teach parents to use the technique themselves with their children. It is part of sensory integration therapy, which is a tool used by occupational therapists to help address sensory and perceptual issues in children with autism.

KEY POINTS AND ADVICE

- Give clear, unambiguous, short instructions.

- Use visual demonstration.

- Offer encouragement and check all is going well.

- Don't expect automatic transfer of information from one task to another.

- Distinguish between phobia and hypersensitivity.

- Enlist the aid of a trained occupational therapist for help with sensory issues or desensitisation programme. They will assess and advise.

- If phobia exists, then see a therapist to address the specific problem.

- If possible, avoid the unwanted excess stimuli to prevent sensory overload.

- Use long-sleeved clothes to protect skin (may not be appropriate for some due to other sensory issues). Emma has been advised that firm-fitting clothing is helpful as it applies gentle all-over pressure, but she doesn't like it. We are all individuals.

EVEN NUMBERS

Dear Diary,

Today has been such a frustrating day. First, I was sitting in the bath relaxing and enjoying myself when I realised I had lost track of time. My bottle of special body soap for those with eczema says to soak for 10 to 20 minutes. So I had to check the time and make sure I hadn't been in the bath longer than the allotted time. So I glanced at the clock and saw it was 9:05am and one second. So then I had to sit and wait until it turned 9:06am because I always get out on an even number. It was annoying because if I had looked at the clock two seconds before, it would have been 9:04am and I could have got straight out. While waiting for the seconds to count down, I noticed the top was off my special soap bottle. By the time I had reached over and got it and done it up and put it back, it had just turned 9:07am. Which meant I had missed 9:06am and now had to wait for 9:08am.

By the time I finally got out the bath I was sure I had been over my allotted 20 minutes and this worried me. Then I put on some music while I got dressed. Well, at least I tried to. Only my volume control seemed to be broken. It kept skipping up in two numbers instead of one. Which would have been fine, except when it turned on, it automatically settled on an odd number volume. So every time I turned it and it went up two, it stayed odd. In the end I gave up. After all, it's better to have no music than to listen to music on an odd number setting.

Then there came dinner time. I love dinner time. I love food. Even though sometimes I forget to have lunch. It's really weird. But moving on. Mum put the food out on trays for us to dish up ourselves as usual. I took my food in even numbers as always. Four smiley faces, four beans and two fishcake halves. Some things Mum only cooks in one – two fishcakes would be a lot – so I have to turn them into two by cutting them in half. I didn't have one fishcake, I had two half fishcakes. Then there was a spare smiley face. I really wanted that smiley face. But it would have given me five smiley faces. So I ate one of my smiley faces, waited a suitable amount of time and then went back and took the spare one, giving me once again four smiley faces.

Only after all this I found a sneaky bean had hidden itself under one of the other beans. So now I had five beans. There were no more beans so I could not make six beans. I stressed about it for ages before finally squishing two beans together and mashing them with my fork so they made one bean. It worked but I still felt icky about it…

Yours,
Emma Louise Bridge

COMMENTARY

In this diary entry Emma has flagged up two situations that caused her issues:

1. following instructions exactly

2. needing to have everything in even numbers.

Following instructions has caused her difficulties not only in this situation but also when cooking with me and when attempting other tasks that have written instructions. It may seem – and in many circumstances it is – a good thing to follow rules and do exactly as is written on the packet, paper, box, etc. But there are times when flexibility is needed and sometimes a task is not achieved and stress levels rise because of lack of ability to be flexible.

I have found that forward planning can reduce stress levels enormously. Ensuring that a suitable even number of items can be provided, or, if not, finding means to adapt what is available, can sometimes avert a crisis. Emma accepts dividing one item into two as an acceptable, though not wholly pleasing, situation. Keeping channels of communication open, discussing issues and talking through is always helpful, so that when situations arise suitable scenarios about how to resolve difficulties will already have been discussed.

I have found that accepting these issues is a necessary part of life, not only for Emma but also for her sister who is on the autistic spectrum too and who shares a love of and need for even numbers.

I have found, however, that I can challenge them in a gentle way where it is not possible to comply exactly to evenness or where flexibility is needed, and we have been able to extend the girls' ability to compromise in some things. This is sometimes a step too far, but it is helpful to extend their abilities and widen their skill set. Emma has good verbal communication and so we can discuss ways of working around problems. Pre-empting situations where I know there will be issues can help to prevent a stressful situation arising in the first place.

KEY POINTS AND ADVICE

- Good forward planning is essential.

- Discussing scenarios and talking through situations beforehand helps people with autism to cope if situations arise.

- I rewrite and edit recipes to give flexibility to allow for necessary changes – for example, cook sausages for 20 minutes; if they are not browned and cooked in the middle, continue to cook for a further six minutes. Repeat this if they are still not cooked.

- It is important to be honest if people outside the family comment when compromises are made – for example, cutting something in half to make two. Stress occurs because others do not realise the importance of this.

- Try to pre-empt situations and be prepared.

MONEY TROUBLES

Dear Diary,

I was having money trouble today. I often have money trouble. My maths is supremely poor. Some people assume because of the autism that my maths and science skills should be amazing, but honestly they are not at all. I keep the calculator on my laptop saved on my start menu because it gets clicked so often. However, this was not bad maths skills today. This was an issue with what I could spend on what. I have some money in my account but it was not for spending. It was being kept for very important necessary things for life. Of course, we don't have to pay for air and Mum covers my food bill. But Mum generally lets me know what else counts as vital for life. If she didn't, I am not sure I would have any money. Thus far, anything with Disney printed on it is apparently not essential for life. I would disagree with that but I am not sure who makes the rules and thus who to disagree with. Plus Mum promised to never knowingly lie to me so I have to trust her on that.

I also had a cheque for my birthday. Now, birthday money I am allowed to spend. However, I couldn't get to the bank to cash the cheque. So when I spotted something I wanted to buy, I didn't know what to do as apparently shops don't just take cheques – trust me on this, I have tried – and I couldn't spend the vitally-important-stuff-for-life money. My mum said that any money I spent from my account would be replaced when I put the birthday money in. She called it 'borrowing from myself' and seemed to think it was fine. I don't really understand it. After all, account money is account money and birthday money is birthday money. You cannot intermix them. I decided to trust her. But I hope I don't get charged interest for this 'borrowing from myself' thing because I heard borrowing money always leaves you owing more interest than money you borrowed.

Yours,
Emma Louise Bridge

COMMENTARY

Rules are rules and not made to be broken. Also, with a mind that does not allow for flexibility or changing the rules, this has led to various difficulties for Emma in life, including the ones she mentions in Entry 6.

The overall issue that arises is following unsaid rules and expectations and knowing what is essential in life or not. In adulthood, as we start to make more decisions, it is difficult to make these choices.

I have found that a solution to help Emma with these difficulties is to have rules put in place which are clear, straightforward and unambiguous. It is important not to rely on unsaid rules or generalised statements which are unhelpful and cause stress and misunderstanding. There should be no expectation that because generally society does things in one way this is acceptable or understood by someone with ASD. Those unsaid rules need to be broken down and made simple to follow.

These rules are very particular to the issues that Emma faces and we make them together. She may not always understand why, but she accepts that these are rules for her own good and she then sticks to them. As we have made them together, she is happy that she has been part of the process. This has been a way of developing her independence in these areas while keeping her from either spending money she did not have or from being too scared to spend any.

It is important to develop trust in the relationship and, as an adult with ASD branches out to more independence, to have others outside the family whom they trust and who can discuss and share these and other issues with them. Especially financial issues such as these.

KEY POINTS AND ADVICE

- Make clear, straightforward, unambiguous rules.

- I make rules with Emma to fill in the gaps where society has unsaid rules that are hard to interpret.

- To develop independence further, increase the number of people outside the family who can be trusted to help and advise if needed.

- Involving Emma in the making of rules means she owns them and accepts them.

OVERWHELMING NOISE

Dear Diary

Today is Sunday and that means church day. It also means Mum cooks at lunchtime instead of dinnertime. Oh and it means that Dad is home. Though he is also home on Saturdays so that's not a Sunday thing. In church everyone was talking at once because the service had not started yet. I kind of felt overwhelmed by all the noise. I have always been sensitive to too much noise. I just cannot stand loud places (or places with more than five people, actually). I felt like I was expected to be saying something but did not know what to say, could not hear what anyone else was saying and did not know who I was expected to be saying something to. Mum started talking to me but I was already panicking. So I just got up and left. I know you are really not supposed to do that, but I couldn't stay so my only option was to leave. I sat outside and rocked for a bit. Rocking back and forth is good because it's comforting and repetitive and makes me feel better.

Back and forth. Back and forth. Back and forth.

Mum and I went and sat on the stairs to one side of the foyer. Someone went and got us both chairs and we watched the service from the safety of there. It was better because there were only two of us and it was quieter, much quieter. A man joined us and that made three, which I didn't like. But then another man joined us and that made four. I didn't really like being in the space with two men, but I did like having the even numbers. We went back into the church for talking after. Well, Mum talked and I hovered awkwardly waiting to go home and feeling stressed again. Well, that and thinking about lunch. I like food and thinking about it makes everything seem a little better. When we got home, Mum ordered me some headphones. When they arrive, I am going to wear them for church to reduce the noise.

Yours,
Emma Louise Bridge

COMMENTARY

As we have mentioned before, hypersensitivity is common in people with ASD and Emma is no exception.

As she explains, the noise level in church was too loud (we have recently moved to a larger new church in a new area), there were too many people and there was the expectation that Emma would have to converse and make small talk with people she did not really know (this in turns brings further difficulties).

Ways we have helped with this situation and continue to do so are:

- We use noise-reduction headphones, especially during the songs.

- It helps to sit somewhere quieter and where she is not surrounded by people.

- As we have been able to move back into the main building, we sit at the back with access to the door for an easy exit if required.

- Emma does not like anyone behind her, so we sit in the back row.

- A family member goes out at the end with her if she wishes to leave straight away, or she stands in a quieter area with family members so she can join in but not feel overwhelmed.

- It has been important to Emma and the family to build up her ability to cope in this type of environment, not only for church but for any gathering where there is noise and a larger number of people than she is comfortable with.

- We take time to build up and do not expect her to adapt quickly.

- We try to ensure that people are aware of the issues so they can support and help her to integrate and do not demand too much from her.

- Prior to any social situation or occasion where a group is involved, it is important to know what to expect and how many people are involved and to explain exactly what is going to happen. This helps to relieve some of the stress even before arriving.

- We have recently developed a sensory bag which can be used in any stressful situation. This contains items which help to de-stress Emma such as anti-stress balls and fiddle pencils.

- Emma does exhibit some behaviours which she finds calming such as rocking – the linear movement helps to provide stress relief – and we do not discourage this as it is her way of independently reducing her stress levels.

JOKING OR LYING?

Dear Diary,

Today I was in one of those situations where everyone laughs and I have no idea what is funny. Actually, I am in those situations a lot. Most of the time it is because I don't understand the joke, rather than I don't find it funny. This is either because I mistake the joke for a lie or because it makes literally no sense to me. See, if someone makes a statement that is obviously untrue, it is a lie. However, if someone makes a statement that is obviously untrue and everyone laughs, then it is a joke. That seems to be the distinction. The question is, what if someone makes a statement that is obviously untrue and expects everyone to laugh, but no one does? Does that make it a lie because no one found it funny? Or is the important thing that it was intended to be funny? Also, if you make a statement that is obviously untrue because you are trying to lie, but everyone laughs even though you were not trying to be funny, is that a joke? Even if the intention was to deceive.

If it is the intention that is important, how are you supposed to know?

These things confuse me. Though other people seem to be confused by it too. Quite often I say something and people laugh even though I wasn't joking. Not lies – lying is bad – just statements that I intend to be a part of the conversation and people laugh at.

Yours,
Emma Louise Bridge

COMMENTARY

The intricacies of human communication, either verbal or non-verbal, is a topic talked a lot about in our household – understanding facial expression, tone of voice, intention behind what is said, whether someone is joking or not and, as Emma says, the difference between joking and lying.

Social skills training and learning to read expression, tone of voice, emotions and so on is helpful, starting at a young age and building on skills learned as children become adults. With the girls, this is not something we were able to do at a young age because we were unaware of their diagnosis. I have taught social skills with children in primary school, however, and so know the benefits of these skills to children's development.

Talking through scenarios and modelling conversations that show what is perceived to be socially acceptable helps to embed these skills so that they become more natural for people with ASD. They can learn to react to and pick up on verbal and non-verbal signals so they can understand better the other person's meaning and pick up on whether they are joking, serious, happy or sad and respond accordingly.

The issue of jokes versus lies is still ongoing as the subtlety of human communication is beyond many of us at times. We continue to discuss situations as they arise and relive conversations to help Emma and her siblings where they have struggled to understand a situation.

KEY POINTS AND ADVICE

- Use social skills training from a young age, as soon as a child is diagnosed.

- Social stories, acting out scenarios and modelling conversations are all helpful.

- Discussing, having open communication where misunderstandings occur, being patient and trying not to take offence are important when someone is accused of lying.

- Emma herself has learned to laugh at appropriate points and then discuss with me later what she didn't understand.

GIVING GIFTS

Dear Diary,

HAPPY BIRTHDAY TO ME! HAPPY BIRTHDAY TO ME! TOTALLY NOT SUNG TO THE COPY-RIGHTED TUNE! HAPPY BIRTHDAY TO ME!

Today it is my birthday. I love birthdays for lots of different reasons. One of these is that only one person is getting presents. We are going out to dinner tonight and I am opening my presents then. That way the whole family gets to be there. While I am thinking about presents, I should probably explain. Events like Christmas are very stressful because everyone has to have a present that elicits the same emotional response or costs the same amount and preferably both. I start getting stressed for Christmas around the end of October onwards. We don't celebrate Halloween, so for me it's straight from my birthday in October to Christmas.

First, it is stressful because people don't like to tell you what they have bought you or how much it cost. So it's impossible to try to guess how much to spend or what to buy in return. This is a dilemma, because if I love my present at Christmas and get all excited and show I love it, and then my mum doesn't love hers and likes it a little, then I have failed in the present-giving tradition and must try harder next year. I should probably note that my other family members insist they do not feel this and they are happy with whatever I get them. But that is beside the point.

On my birthday it does not matter because only I am getting presents. Though I do find it hard to get super-excited, even if I love my gift, because if I get super-excited by one gift, then the other gifts might not get the same response and that would be unfair. However, getting super-excited by all the gifts would be super-tiring. Plus I might not love all the gifts the same. But if I don't get super-excited about any gifts, then that is mean to the people buying me the gift. But how do you get super-excited about your favourite gifts while making sure the other gifts know that you love them too and they won't be abandoned in a cupboard somewhere? I know inanimate objects cannot love you, but you can love them and I wouldn't want my love to be shared out unevenly. After all, love is being pleased to see something, isn't it, and I am always pleased to see my things.

Yours,
Emma Louise Bridge

COMMENTARY

We have tried to help Emma with her dilemma with the receiving and giving of presents by making a rule of how much the family will spend and then also making a list each of a few items that we would like to be given. We all have the same amount and we know what we are getting is something we want, but it is still a surprise as it is chosen by the giver from the list. This can be extended to friends, although that is not possible when a gift is unexpected. Forward planning and the cooperation of those involved is necessary, but it does save a lot of stress.

We have helped Emma to be able to show pleasure on receiving a gift – especially when it is from outside the family or from extended family – through social skills training and modelling behaviours, so even if she does not feel great excitement, she can respond appropriately and the giver feels appreciated. She does not have to leap around but can say or show that she appreciates the gift.

Certain stock phrases are useful to remember if she doesn't know what to say.

KEY POINTS AND ADVICE

- Each member of the family makes a gift list with a few items for the others to choose.

- Where possible, set the amount of money each family member will spend, although there will always be surprises when unexpected gifts are received.

- Forward planning can help to reduce the number of awkward and stressful surprises.

- Modelling behaviour to show pleasure and express gratitude can be helpful, especially when the recipient of a gift is stuck for words.

- We have some stock phrases for Emma to use when she is unsure what to say in order to respond without giving offence.

OWNERSHIP

Dear Diary,

Ownership is a very funny thing. I spent a lot of today thinking about it. I have a lot of free time because of how hard it is for me to leave the house and interact with others. I have been thinking about the ownership dilemma since I got my presents actually. If someone gives you a present, then that belongs to you as long as you have it. But the person has let you have it as gift to you and not to anyone else. So if you don't want the gift any more or don't need the gift any more, then you cannot give it away. You have to give it back. I struggle with this when it comes to money too. If someone gives me money, then I want to spend it on something they would approve of because it's their money. So I have to think about what I am buying and make sure I don't buy anything they wouldn't want me to buy.

In the same way, if you buy someone else a present, you buy it for them specifically. If they don't want it any more, they should give it back to you. As you are the one who decided to give it to them, you are the one who should decide what happens to it next. Unless you have given them permission to do whatever they like with it. Or they have given you permission to do whatever you like. It would be rather difficult to track down everyone who has ever given me something. I feel bad about it. I should probably have kept a list. Especially since we had to give away a lot of stuff recently. Stuff that by rights should have been returned to whoever gave it to me because they did not specifically tell me I had permission to gift it to charity.

Yours,
Emma Louise Bridge

COMMENTARY

The problem that Emma describes is one of ownership. We have approached this from the standpoint that a gift is something one person gives to another. It is free to the person receiving it and it becomes theirs to do with as they wish. Because it is free to them, it is also free for them to use and then give away as they see fit when they no longer want it. This also includes a gift of money. Although this is still a problem for Emma, she has come to accept this principle and it has made things easier for her.

KEY POINTS AND ADVICE

- › When a gift is given, it is free and comes with permission for that person to keep it and use it as they see fit. This is also true when receiving a gift.

- › Having talked through it with us, Emma has eventually accepted this principle.

- › When items are part of an obsession, this becomes more difficult – those things are not parted with until the obsession passes and is replaced by another one.

- › In some cases, items from an obsession have been boxed up and stored because it is too difficult to pass them on, but it has been accepted in advance by Emma that they will no longer be present in the bedroom. Space is then made for new items.

THEY ALREADY KNOW

Dear Diary,

One day in secondary school we had to do this big colouring project. It was meant to be a map of the world. We had to work in pairs to do it. I found my half of the map in a box of old stuff when I was going through my room today. It wasn't very good so I didn't keep it. However, I remember drawing it really well. I don't remember many incidents from school. I try not to. Some have really stuck with me over the years, though.

It was me and this other girl – I will call her Anna in case she reads this – and we were using my colouring pencils. When we were done, she put the pencils away in their box and put them in her bag. Then she went up to hand in our map. I realised she must have forgotten we were using my pencils. I took them out her bag and put them away in my bag where they belonged. Then I finished packing everything up. When she came back, she was putting stuff in her bag and suddenly announced the pencils were gone. She was looking everywhere for them.

I was just leaving when she asked me where the pencils were. I told her they were in my bag. She got all cross because I hadn't told her sooner, even though she hadn't asked me. I pointed out she knew they were in my bag because I knew they were in my bag – so why wouldn't she? She just stared at me and grumbled that she'd been handing the map in. She then marched off.

Now that I think back on the incident, I can kind of see where she was coming from. I mean I don't understand why she was mad, but it has since been explained to me that people don't know everything I know. That, and you have to tell people information even though they don't ask for it.

I guess bullies were not the only reason school was difficult. Some things just didn't make sense. I suppose we don't have to make sense of everything. It would be nice if we could, though.

Yours,
Emma Louise Bridge

COMMENTARY

Theory of mind is an understanding that a person has thoughts, feelings and beliefs that they hold and an understanding that other people have feelings, thoughts and beliefs that may be different to your own. People on the autistic spectrum struggle with theory of mind and often think that because they are feeling or thinking something everyone else must feel and think or believe the same.

I have encouraged Emma to say how she is feeling or to tell us if something is really bothering her, even though she thinks we already know. She has accepted this rule even though her assumption remains the same. She will tell us not only her feelings but also if something has happened that we need to be aware of.

She does need reminding to do so on occasions.

KEY POINTS AND ADVICE

- Expressing feelings verbally should be encouraged, even if they think people already know.

- Although Emma knows she has to tell people things she thinks they should already know, this has not come naturally. It was taught and she needs reminding.

- If verbal communication is difficult, then use visual images to present different emotions.

- With the pencils issue, Emma now understands that she should have said she had taken them. When scenarios arise, use them to develop understanding and then work on that skill for further situations.

- Sometimes a skill is learned even if the underlying belief doesn't change. Emma accepted she needed to share this type of information even though she didn't see why.

THEY ARE ALL
THE SAME

Dear Diary,

I was reading an article today. I end up reading a lot of random articles because I get drawn in to fun links on the internet and end up clicking on anything that flashes at me. I had to put parental control on the laptop just for safety because of this. Anyway, in this article the person was talking about people with autism being exactly the same. I am not sure how this is possible. Most people I know with autism are boys – it's a condition predominantly found in boys – and I am most definitely a girl. I have checked. So this is something different for a start. But if the article meant personality and quirks being the same, that doesn't make sense either. My sister and I both have autism but we are nothing alike.

She is scared of horses but I love horses. Bugs make me scream and run for the house, but she tolerates them, except for spiders. My sister and I both like even numbers, but even in that we differ because she says number one is all right because it's a single number, but I think number one doesn't count because it's odd. Also 27 is her lucky number even though it's odd, and my lucky number, which I haven't actually chosen, would have to be even. So how can we all be the same? I mean, I understand thinking that everyone thinks and feels what everyone else is thinking and feeling. That's having difficulties with theory of mind, apparently. But people tell me that everyone doesn't actually know what I am thinking. I just think they do.

If everyone with autism was the same, that would be a lot of sameness. It would be like an army of clones. I have watched enough TV to know armies of clones are never good. They always come right before someone attempts to take over the world. I am not sure I would want to be used in someone's world domination plans. Me and my best friend at school had world domination plans. We were going to be benevolent dictators. We were much younger then, though, and strangely our plan did not actually involve an army of clones.

Yours,
Emma Louise Bridge

P.S. Going to write to the author of the article and ask them to answer my questions.

COMMENTARY

Emma has flagged up the all too frequent situation of stereotyping of people on the autistic spectrum.

Each child/adult is an individual and should be treated as such. In order for a diagnosis to be made, there must be the triad of impairments in social behaviour, imagination and communication, but how each individual expresses those will vary tremendously. That is why it is called the autistic *spectrum*. Also there is a multitude of sensory/perceptual issues involved in autism which many would say are key to the whole condition.

In her diary entry, Emma cites the differences between her and her sister. They have the same diagnosis, but although they think the same in some areas, they have very different views, sensitivities and challenges in others.

There is also the challenge that parents with girls face because ASD is predominantly seen as a male condition and, as we know as parents, it is harder for girls to obtain a diagnosis. Our girls were not diagnosed until 19 and 23 years old, and this did not happen through the educational system, although in Emma's sister's case there were many more pointers to indicate to us that she was on the spectrum far earlier.

There are many reasons why autism is not picked up in girls, including their ability to mimic behaviour better than boys and the fact that the types of games they play fit in with those of non-autistic girls; they also tend to be less disruptive than boys, and they may be drawn to girls who will mother them and so they are socially protected. But as they get older, especially reaching secondary school with the increase in changes of routine, stimuli and peer groups, the challenges they face increase, the autistic traits become more apparent and their ability to cope can diminish. Also mental illness such as depression and anxiety can cloud the issue, as it did with Emma. Grades at school can start to fall which leads to increased anxiety and stress. This was our experience as a family.

Because girls can show signs of ASD in a different way to boys, it is vital that more is understood about these differences and that parents and teachers and professionals are aware and more able to see the signs. Earlier diagnosis, intervention and support can then be put in place to help those children in all aspects of their development and help their parents who otherwise can be left to cope alone.

KEY POINTS AND ADVICE

- Everyone is an individual and should be treated as such. There is no such thing as a typical 'autistic person'. They may have the same diagnosis but will have very different needs (as you will already know). Don't expect something that helps with one will necessarily help with another.

- Within a family there may be jealousy. At times more help is needed by one member than another and it is important that all feel they are being equally supported. It is a juggling act trying to accommodate the needs of everyone, but to be seen to be doing so helps. When more time is given to one, try to explain and help the others to understand why.

- It helps to spend a small amount of one-to-one time with each child if possible.

- Allow everyone to unload feelings to relieve tensions.

- Try not to compare siblings on the spectrum. They will be different.

- As parents, if you are at all concerned about your child but can't put your finger on why, do not hesitate to express those concerns to your GP or the school. This is especially true for girls who may well be overlooked and not picked up.

- Girls do present differently. Be informed and read information from the internet, books or ask about the differences and what to look for.

- We have found a diagnosis opens the door to support that is not there otherwise. This goes for older children and young adults especially with help at university/college and entry to the work place.

THE
'HOW ARE YOU?'
QUESTION

Dear Diary,

I had such a confusing conversation today. Of course, a lot of conversations are confusing for me. But today it was when someone asked me how I was. In the past I used to answer this question with my entire life story or at least a record of what I was feeling and had been feeling for the last week, month… However, people tended to complain. Also, if I am having a bad day, then I generally assume everyone else must know I am having a bad day because they must be having a bad day too. After all, everyone thinks and feels the same; they just don't all know it. So back to the person who had asked me. I didn't want to say I was fine because I am not. I am tired and I have a headache and being outside the house was stressing me out.

So I just kind of looked at the person blankly. Then they looked back at me for a while and it was really quiet. I hate the quiet because it gives me too much time to think. If I think too much, then I give myself more stuff to worry about. The list can be endless if it goes on too long. On the other hand, if neither of us is talking, then neither of us is saying the wrong thing and I like that. I finally told them I was tired and then left it at that. As long as they didn't ask me why I was tired, the conversation was done. They then looked back at me expectantly. I could not for the life of me work out what they wanted. It turns out they wanted me to ask 'How are you?' back.

Now, I have a problem with this. First, they should have told me that is what they wanted. Second, I feel I should only have to ask 'How are you?' if I actually want to know how someone is. Otherwise it's basically lying because you are deceiving the other person into thinking you care how they are. Sometimes I care how people are and sometimes I just want to know they are not dead or in horrific pain and that's enough. I am not sure why you would expect anything more from someone you care about, and if you don't care about them, why would you want to know anyway? Some people seem to ask the question purely because they are supposed to and not because they want to listen to an answer – and so why do those people deserve a response?

Yours,
Emma Louise Bridge

COMMENTARY

'How are you?' should be a very easy question but it can cause a lot of difficulties for those with ASD. How should they respond to this question? How much should they say? What should they say? Should they say anything at all? And then, in return, do they ask 'How are you?' back?

We have discussed these questions at great length and found that teaching Emma a set formula for responding usually helps her to be able to respond to the initial question of 'How are you?' with a suitable response – which is not just 'Fine' as this she regards as not true (unless she is fine). She responds with a statement such as 'I am a bit tired' and hopes this will end the conversation.

We talked through several of these short responses suitable for how she is feeling.

We have also taught Emma to ask 'How are you?' in return. Even if she may not want to know the answer, she feels this has helped her fit in and feel more comfortable in these situations.

Again, this is where social skills training, modelling conversations and preparing in advance for social situations is helpful.

KEY POINTS AND ADVICE

» We have taught Emma a stock of replies suitable for occasions when she is unsure of how to respond.

» Use social skills training and modelling conversations to demonstrate how to interact in these situations and what sort of questions to ask in response.

» Responding with appropriate phrases is socially acceptable and helps Emma to fit in.

» People like talking about themselves and it reduces the amount of talking Emma has to do if she is listening. This is a good skill to learn.

THE DILEMMA
OF TIMING

Dear Diary,

I love my family to bits, but today they were driving me crazy. I don't know if that is possible. It might be one of those things people say that makes no sense. Like the other day, my friend said 'sweating like a pig on heat' when everyone knows that pigs don't sweat. I try to avoid using phrases like that because they just don't make sense. So anyway I was getting stressed. My family just would not pick a time for leaving. I had this appointment and I wanted to know exactly what time I was leaving. Finally they picked a time. Except, as far as I am concerned, leaving at a certain time means that is the time you walk out the door. Not that is the time you start putting your shoes on. Because we said that was the time we were leaving. They should have said that is the time we were putting our shoes on if that is what they meant.

Admittedly, timing is difficult. I absolutely hate being late for things. I would rather be super-early than even a minute late. But my mum pointed out to me the other day that some people don't like you being too early for things. After all, there might be an appointment before mine or something else the person is doing. So really you want to be exactly on time. Except that is almost impossible to do. Plus my appointment is at the top of three flights of stairs. I arrive and get buzzed in and walk up the steps. So if I arrive at the door at the exact time of my appointment, then by the time I have walked up the three flights of stairs I am late. However, if I arrive early, then I disturb the person while they might be in another appointment, but by the time I have walked the three flights of stairs I am on time.

I don't know why people don't make rules for these things. Society seems to have all these rules but no one lets me know any of the important ones. There should just be sets of times. For example, when leaving the house you should decide a putting-on-shoes time and a leaving time, not just a leaving time. In the same way, if I have an appointment involving stairs, there should be an arriving-at-the-bottom-of-the-stairs time and an appointment-actually-starting time, pre-decided. That way everyone would be on the same page and nobody would be late.

Yours
Emma Louise Bridge

P.S. Still trying to locate the rule book that covers society's predetermined rules that I don't know.

COMMENTARY

A need for routines, schedules and exact timekeeping is common for people with ASD. Emma expresses her difficulties with being early or late and also with getting others to comply with her need to be precise.

It is hard because not everyone fits into these carefully laid plans and this causes stress.

This is an issue that we have attempted to address as a family. We try to be clear about our intentions and keep to a schedule, taking into account Emma's needs. We make sure everyone knows timings of appointments and we plan accordingly to ensure we are not late. Any changes in routine need to be talked through first and explained.

KEY POINTS AND ADVICE

* Be definite about plans and stick to them.

* Write down all appointments and work back so enough time is left to get there and also to prepare to leave the house (which always takes longer than we think).

* Talk through any changes in routine or why things are different.

* Try not to make sudden changes without warning.

* Planning and discipline are essential.

PEOPLE CAN BE
SO SCARY

Dear Diary,

I decided to go on a little walk today. It has been advised that walking would be good for me. Plus I don't go out the house by myself often because of my social anxiety. So every now and then it is good to test myself and attempt a short walk alone. My destination of choice was the local shop. Nice short walk, food at the end – perfect.

The walk started off okay. It was a little stressful being out, but it was bearable. Except after a few moments I spotted a guy walking towards me. So I instantly hurried to cross the road (though in a safe way), which was stressful in itself because it wasn't crossing at the crossing I like to use every time we go to the local shop. Plus it turned out on the other side of the road there was a man sitting in his van with the door open. Now both people are potentially nice people with no interest whatever in what I was doing. Of course, they are both potentially not nice people either. I have met nice people and not nice people in my time. I would rather assume that someone is not nice and be safe than assume someone is nice and regret it.

Except this left me with a bit of a dilemma. I didn't know what either guy was doing. In the end, I had to flatten myself against the hedge, edge slowly past the van and then run for a bit. Problem temporarily solved, even if I am feeling breathless and my chest hurts, so I can at least finally make it to the shop. Inside the shop the staff were all busy out on the floor, so even when the time came for me to pay there was no one to serve me. The people must have been aware they were not at the counter, as they were spread out over the shop, and I did not want to tell people something obvious. So I stood and waited till finally someone turned up to let me pay. It was awkward and stressful, but approaching someone would have been worse.

The way home was pretty similar. The guy in the van was still there, and there was another man on the other side of the road still. Oh and near the end I heard someone running up behind me later on the route. I almost fainted. It was so scary! He ran past me, though, and off down the road, leaving me to run home and then sit in the corner rocking and crying.

When the going gets tough, the tough panic and run home as fast as their unfit legs will carry them.

Yours,
Emma Louise Bridge

COMMENTARY

Emma suffers from severe social anxiety. She rarely leaves the house on her own; if she does, it is for a short trip which is planned in advance.

There are several reasons for the anxiety, only some of which are related to the autism; the other reasons are situational from past experiences that have affected her life.

It is really important to understand where the social anxiety comes from and also whether seeking medical intervention is appropriate.

Research seems to suggest that what is often classed as a 'meltdown' can, in autistic adults, actually be social anxiety; it can therefore be addressed differently and the help given changed accordingly.

We are all aware of Emma's need to gradually build her self-confidence and her ability to go out alone and so we plan trips that she feels should succeed. We talk through scenarios which may happen on the way and ways of coping with different situations if they arise. On her return, if, as on this particular trip, there were stresses, when the initial panic is over, we talk through how she could cope next time.

Starting with very small achievable goals is helpful, and breaking down tasks into chunks so the whole is not overwhelming means success is more likely. Then it is important to build on each success as it happens.

An example of a small step was to go into a shop together and then for Emma to look at items on her own and purchase one at the till. I was present but at a distance. This gave her confidence but also some independence.

KEY POINTS AND ADVICE

- Always set achievable goals.

- Start small and slowly add on further challenges as each step is mastered.

- Don't worry if there are days when things go backwards; it will happen. There are some days when Emma doesn't attempt things because they are just too difficult, but on others she can cope.

- Plan everything in advance.

- Talk through scenarios that might happen and how to overcome them if they do. Limit the number of scenarios – you could be talking for ever and it could cause more stress. Focus on the most important ones.

- There is a difference between a panic attack and a 'meltdown'.

- With a panic attack, Emma has a technique of finding her happy place and imagining she is a shark (she loves sharks). She can then focus away from what she is panicking about and it helps her to relax.

• With social anxiety, facing her fears in a controlled and gradual way is helping her to overcome them.

• If there is any underlying cause for the social anxiety, this can be a focus in helping to overcome it.

• Seek medical help, therapy and support where appropriate.

• It is important that those providing medical help, therapy and support understand the needs of someone with ASD and can work with them, taking those needs into account.

CROSSING THE ROAD AND SHARING THE PAVEMENT

Dear Diary,

Today I was faced with three highly difficult situations. I am aware these are really first-world problems. I am not starving and I am not dying, so really whether I can leave the house or not… well, yeah, it still seems to matter whether I can leave the house or not. First, we were walking into town as a group and we had to cross the road. The others all crossed but I can't cross if there is a car coming, even if it's in the distance. Especially if, like now, there was no pre-assigned crossing place. A car was coming so I didn't cross, but then the car slowed down. So I moved forward, but the car didn't stop so I backed off. Then they gestured for me to cross – at least I think that is what they were saying; they could have been waving or doing anything – so I hovered back and forth and then ran across the road anyway.

Safely on the other side, the walk continued. We had to across another road, but this time there was a pre-assigned crossing. The light was red so we waited. No cars were coming so some of my companions crossed the road. I just waited. Whether there are cars on the road is irrelevant if the red man is standing still. So finally the red man goes to the green man and I managed to cross the road. Some people say you can walk when there are no cars even if it's red, but these are crazy people. The red man is for standing still.

Finally, we got to the part where most of the people are. I was by this point already trying to remember why I was forcing myself to endure all this. Especially when it came to the art of overtaking on the pavement. I got trapped behind someone walking too slowly for me to walk comfortably. This is really pretty slow. If I overtook them, however, I would have had to keep walking fast and pay attention constantly to whether I was slowing down or not. After all, the person has watched you overtake them. Therefore they know you wanted to walk faster, so you can't suddenly change your mind. I am sure this is one of those social rules, though no one has told me as such. Just like when you're driving and you overtake someone, you can't then decide to go slowly afterwards. The problem is, the more I check my pace, the slower I end up going.

Yours,
Emma Louise Bridge

COMMENTARY

As we have seen before, a rule is a rule and rules are not to be broken. Like crossing the road when the red man is showing. We teach our children to be safe crossing the road and usually we do not cross unless the green man is showing. Emma is right in this, and it is the rest of us who need to be more consistent.

Crossing the road where there is no designated crossing is more challenging and relies on making judgements about what the car drivers are doing. Modelling what to do, talking through and having some simple rules to follow can help.

KEY POINTS AND ADVICE

- We stick to the rules and cross at a crossing (where possible) and wait for the green man before we walk.

- Where a crossing is not available, use a gradual approach to develop independence: modelling, accompanying, first showing and then allowing them, where appropriate, to take the lead.

- Ensure that simple guidelines are understood.

- Plan the route in advance if possible so that any difficulties have already been foreseen and thought about.

BEDTIME PALS

Dear Diary,

Bedtime pals – pals used for bedtime. Usually fluffy or squishy, aka nice to cuddle.

I have two main bedtime pals. I know by my age most people don't have bedtime pals. However, I love my bedtime pals. Besides, I am uncomfortable at night and often have nightmares. I have a vivid imagination and my nightmares can often be highly graphic. Definitely come with an 18 warning. This is despite reassurances from my family that kidnappers don't work on Sundays or Friday nights, wouldn't be able to fit through my window and probably aren't around anyway, because the number of kidnappers working today is remarkably small. My light is one with a dimmer switch so that I can leave it on at night, and I have my bedtime pals.

One is a ginger cat in an army uniform called 'Prince Harry'. He gets called 'PH' for short because people thought I was really weird when I was talking about how 'Prince Harry' kept falling out of bed last night. (No offence to the real Prince

Harry, who I think is awesome.) The other is a ginger cat in a Thor costume called 'Thor'. I had to use the Marvel Comics Thor outfit because that is what was available. He is based on the original Thor, though, because the original Norse god was ginger. I love Marvel but it's not quite the same as the original. I had one bedtime pal for years and that was 'Prince Harry'. Then I decided to start my famous-redheads-through-history collection and 'Thor' arrived.

When he arrived, I had to snuggle them both at the same time. However, this got really uncomfortable because I roll around in my sleep a lot and two bedtime pals kept getting in the way. So I switched to just snuggling 'Thor'. But then I felt I was abandoning my original bedtime pal, 'Prince Harry'. However, when I switched to just snuggling him, I felt that was making my 'Thor', as the new bedtime pal, feel unwanted and unloved. I spent a lot of time at school feeling that. (Not at home. Home was awesome. School sucked.) So I didn't want 'Thor' to feel this way. So after worrying about what to do and not getting any sleep, I finally came up with a solution.

I now have a snuggle-time schedule. It's fair and even and makes sure that everyone gets enough snuggle time. Writing a schedule to make sleep-time easy actually kept me awake most of the night, but for every other night I am now sorted.

Yours,
Emma Louise Bridge

COMMENTARY

Emma found a solution to her problem herself and is now happy with her snuggle-time schedule.

IN ITS PLACE

Dear Diary,

Today I was giving all my new presents a place in my room. I know it's been a few days since my birthday but it's a very stressful process giving things a proper home. Once the home has been assigned, it cannot be undone. Therefore it is a lot pressure to get it right. This got me thinking about the trauma of moving house. To be honest, that is never far from my mind nowadays. You see, in my old room at our old house everything had a place and everything fit exactly in its place. If I was reading a book and had to pop to answer the phone or go to the loo, then the book would be returned to its place even though I was going to come back for it a short while later.

Now the problem is that in my new room in the new house I had to give everything a new place. However, no matter what place I gave it, it was in the wrong place because it wasn't in its pre-assigned place. Its pre-assigned place is four hours away in the old house. We haven't sold that house yet, though we are trying to, and so the places for my stuff are still sitting there back in that house, waiting for my stuff. In my new room nothing ever feels right because it isn't the right place. The sooner we can sell our old house and buy a new one the better. I was going to try to keep everything in its assigned temporary box space until that happened. Except I don't physically have the space to live out of boxes.

So now I am faced with the dilemma of what to do with my stuff…

Yours,
Emma Louise Bridge

P.S. My birthday presents were never in the old house. But I can't assign them places when nothing else has a place.

COMMENTARY

When we were preparing to move house, we needed to help Emma and her sister prepare for the changes that were ahead. Especially as we were going into a rented house. Their rooms were very special to them and a place of sanctuary and escape.

Both girls handled the move in different ways. With Emma, we involved her in all things, being aware at times if it got too much for her and the stress levels went too high. Her sister didn't want to be involved at all. This shows how they are individuals even though they both have ASD.

There were a lot of changes in the house and this caused stress.

In order to prepare for a new room, Emma took a step forward and had her room in our old house painted a new colour. This was a step towards change before the major change of moving happened. It was hard but it started the process of disassociating her from the house and her room and preparing her for the fact that her new room would be a different.

Now in their new rooms, her sister has adopted the living-from-boxes idea; although it is still a struggle, she has accepted that our situation is for a short time and in her permanent room she will have a place for everything. Emma has rearranged many times but has found a temporary but acceptable solution. She still looks on our old house as ours and that room as hers, but when it is sold that issue will be resolved.

KEY POINTS AND ADVICE

- It's essential to accept that major life changes such as moving house are going to be extra stressful.

- Try to prepare for the change by finding ways to disassociate from the old to move on to the new – such as Emma's change of room colour.

- Work with individual children in ways that best suit them –for example, if they need to be very involved, then give them jobs and make them feel part of the process and helpful. If they cannot engage, then it is important to accept that this may not happen until the move actually takes place.

- We found it important not to say anything concrete or definite unless we were absolutely sure it was going to happen.

- If there is going to be a change in plan, ensure it is explained and try to prepare ahead if possible so it doesn't come as a surprise.

- We did not anticipate Emma's feelings about the old house while it is not sold and so needed to adapt our support for her.

- Try to make the new environment as calming and structured for their things as possible. New items of storage and furniture can help to accommodate treasured possessions in a different-shaped room. New is not always 'bad'. If it is 'new', it has not had an assigned place yet so that it can be assimilated (based on Emma's words).

- As the situation is fluid, we have to adapt and alter our strategies and help the girls to do the same when unavoidable changes happen.

- Emma constantly changes her room at the moment – moving furniture and items. This is just her way of coping with our situation, and we have to be patient and accepting.

- Emma has just purchased a new bookcase to fit her collections of DVDs and CDs and she is happier they have a place now. She will take this to the new house so it will remain the same when we move again.

THE ART OF
CLEARING

Dear Diary,

Today I continued with sorting out my bedroom. As my new room has less space than my old bedroom, I logically need less stuff. Which means periodically purging my stuff. However, clearing is not easy. First, I have to find anything that was given to me as a present and put it in a pile. In my earlier entry about presents I explained this. These are things I cannot give away. Then everything I love is added to the keep pile. Then anything Mum had agreed is necessary for a happy life goes in the keep pile. Then everything I have not got my money's worth out of – and therefore would feel like it was a waste of money if I gave it away – goes in the keeping pile. Then everything left is to be given away. Except I take out anything that needs to be thrown away. Then make sure there is absolutely nothing related to my favourite things, mentioned below, in the pile. By this point there is very little left in the giving-away pile.

I suppose the things that I don't feel I have got my money's worth out of should still be given away because whoever gets them next will use them. However, they would be paying extra money for them. A separate amount so it's different. I have also been told that I shouldn't keep things just because they are related to my favourite things (see next entry for full list). Though I disagree. I think getting rid of any part of a collection is bad.

Yours,
Emma Louise Bridge

COMMENTARY

Emma has a problem with giving away her things even when it is necessary. As she explains, there are a number of reasons why this is difficult for her.

Because of the move it has been necessary to do some clearing and this has been very challenging for her and her sister. I have found the only way is to do it together, looking at each item and making a decision on each one and its merits. I have had to be firm but have a reason that is acceptable to them if items need to be passed on.

When we have given items to raise money for charity, Emma has found this acceptable as she feels it has been done for a good cause.

KEY POINTS AND ADVICE

- When it is necessary to give away items, go through them together and look at each one in turn and make a decision. I have had to be firm at times or nothing would have been given away.

- Once a decision has been made, we have found it needs to be acted on straight away or the items will not remain for very long in the giving-away pile.

- Sometimes placing items in a box and storing them out of sight is a first step to removing them completely.

- Items that belong to a collection or are part of an obsession are much more difficult to give away. Be sensitive to this and don't expect them to be able to part with them easily. We have found breaking up sets – for example, of books or DVDs – is not acceptable. It is all or nothing.

- Even giving to charity can cause problems, as we found when my other daughter wanted to retrieve all the things she had given away. Time and patience was the only thing that sorted that one.

OBSESSIONAL PERSONALITY

Dear Diary,

Today I was feeling like a staying-at-home day. I was out a lot yesterday and after I have been out a lot I like to be home. I was also in a film-marathon kind of mood. I put on one of my Disney films and settled down for the long haul. You see, when you have an obsessional personality like mine, the things you like very quickly become the things you love. For example, I start by buying the Horrible Histories book set. Then it's the CDs. Then it's the DVD box set. Then the games. Suddenly, you are standing at the till with something just because it has 'Horrible Histories' written on it. Don't get me wrong, I love all that stuff I just mentioned. It just gets a little difficult when you love stuff that much.

Currently my list of favourite things is: the Minions (including the two *Despicable Me* films), Disney, Horrible Histories, the Monarchy and Harry Potter. With secondary favourites being: Sharks, Marvel and History (Ancient–WWII).

I don't like to grade things because it makes me feel bad, so to clarify the second group is merely secondary because I can spot something related to one of those in a shop and make myself leave it even if I have the money. The first list, Mum has to make me leave it behind. She's good at being strong, though, and I am grateful for it because it means when I do get stuff it's more special.

Because of my personality and because it's so hard to see the big picture, I have a hard time with collections. Mostly because the moment I have one thing I want everything else and straight away. In fact, I want everything to do with the collection the second it becomes important to me. It's mainly because I cannot see what's going to happen in the future. The fact I might get something next week means nothing to me. I just see it that if I don't get my entire collection instantly, I won't get it. Like when I give my hamster a pile of food and she eats it all immediately because she cannot comprehend that tomorrow she might want some of that food. I am trying to be strong, though. Recently I got a history book which I love and it's one of a collection of books. Since I have got all the Biggles books I could find, I needed a new book collection. However, I am working really hard on waiting and only getting the books when I can afford it and not all at once, so it actually lasts.

You know what almost got bumped to the first list? Sharks. I mean, I like misunderstood animals in general but mostly sharks. For my birthday last year a friend got me a shark hat that looks like a shark's eating my head. I also have a Minion hat with gloves that I got from my sister. Today we were going on a trip out as a family – bar my sister – and it was cold out so I wanted to wear a hat. I chose my shark hat. But my brother was highly embarrassed and begged me to wear the Minion hat. I got outside and my dad said the Minion hat was more embarrassing and he liked the shark hat. My brother said he didn't want to come if I wore the shark hat. So I was left with a dilemma. In the end I decided it's cold, the shark hat I like best. So I wore the shark hat. As it was someone told me how much they liked it in town.

Shark hat – 1

Minion hat – 0

Yours,
Emma Louise Bridge

COMMENTARY

In this entry Emma talks about her obsessive personality, which leads her to collect things and want everything at once.

She also mentions the shark hat vs Minion hat dilemma and the reaction of the family to those items of headwear.

It seems to me that this was about self-esteem and Emma being able to express herself in the way she chooses. We had a big family discussion about this dilemma and it raised a very important issue: to be confident in yourself and who you are and not worry about what other people think, but at the same time fit into society and not be laughed at for your choice of unusual apparel or behaviour. On this occasion a lady commented on the hat and how much she liked it, and Emma felt vindicated in her choice.

In order to make friends and join in, people need to learn to follow some social 'norms', but I think we can push them too far sometimes in an attempt to help them fit it and try to change inherently who they are. It is a fine line between helping them to follow society's rules and allowing and encouraging them to have freedom of expression to be who they are no matter how 'quirky' that may be.

As my girls were growing up, being 'different' caused them difficulties and problems with friendships and fitting in, but trying to conform and change has also brought its difficulties.

Many people collect items, some to an extreme, having everything related to that subject no matter what it is. Emma's issue is wanting it now. Money can be spent quickly and unwisely to fulfil this need. As she says, we have rules about what is needed, what is acceptable and what can wait. I do have to be firm and am teaching her and her sister to resist the temptation to just buy, even if they do not see the benefits of not doing so at the time. With the books Emma is collecting, she has lists of all of those published and she has bought a boxed set and is now reading those before she is allowed to go on to looking to purchase more.

KEY POINTS AND ADVICE

> • Accept people for who they are and don't expect or demand they change because they don't fit into the 'norms' of society.

> • We all have issues. The shark vs Minion hat issue was in part related to other family members' fears and embarrassment rather than to Emma having a problem.

> • There are times when it is necessary to gently advise and suggest when a change in appearance (especially where hygiene is related) would be beneficial to prevent your child/young adult

from being the brunt of embarrassing comments or laughter. This is very individual and should be handled sensitively.

- Building self-esteem and encouraging them to develop their own personality and strengths is really important.

- Have rules for collections – how much, how many, time frame, etc. Make the rules realistic and the time frame acceptable. Having lists or a plan as a visual timetable is easier to stick to.

- Be firm about not allowing extra or added things unless it's for a particular reason – for example, a birthday gift or doing jobs to earn money to buy another item.

BUT WE AREN'T

Dear Diary,

We saw a woman out in town today. Well, I saw a woman. She had this really old-fashioned sort of backpack and a bicycle. She had this really weird-looking bundle tied to the bike too. When I got home, I went online and was telling my friend about her. I said about how maybe she was a secret spy disguised as a homeless person. Or perhaps she was from the past and had been transported with only a few belongings and no idea how to get home. My friend told me that maybe the woman thought the same thing about me.

Except I told her the same thing my sister told my mum when they had a similar conversation – the woman wouldn't think that about me because I am not one of those things. Then my friend said that woman isn't either of those things. I told her she might be. Then she said that I might be one of those things just the same. Except that is stupid because I am not. I know I am not one of those things. The woman knows I am not one of those things. Then my friend said the woman knows she's not, but she can't know she's not because she might be. That debate went on for quite some time until my friend gave up.

I am going to Google search the possibility of time travel and homeless spy costumes.

Yours,
Emma Louise Bridge

COMMENTARY

I have had this discussion with both my daughters and still have found it difficult to explain. It returns to the problem with theory of mind which means that an autistic person thinks that another person must think and feel the same as them or know what they know.

In Emma's mind, the lady on the bike would know Emma was not a spy or time traveller, because she wasn't.

KEY POINTS AND ADVICE

- This is an ongoing issue and when it arises I remind the girls that they cannot make the assumption that the other person knows, feels, thinks the same as they do.

- Endless discussion is fruitless. In the end, acceptance that this is how it is seems to be the way forward.

- As mentioned in a previous entry, stating what seems to be obvious is a way to ensure people do know what you are thinking or feeling even if you don't feel you should have to tell them.

ADVERTS

Dear Diary,

Watching adverts on TV can be such a traumatic experience nowadays. I watched an advert today about Marmite. I was watching some programme beforehand about something or other and it came on. The poor little neglected and abandoned Marmite pots were being collected from houses that were not eating them and taken to shelters – where they would be chosen by new families who would use them as they are supposed to. I almost cried when the family picked out the little Marmite pot and he got to be loved and enjoyed. It made me want to rush out and buy every pot of Marmite in the world, even though I don't like the taste, and make sure my dad, who does like the taste, ate all of them to make them feel loved and know they have fulfilled their life purpose.

See, I don't really have the money to be spending on excessive pots of Marmite. However, with my literal mind and my inability to say no to people, adverts have that reaction a lot. A poverty advert will reduce me to tears, but so will an advert with a sad-looking cartoon animal asking you to buy whatever product they're selling. Any advert with a tune that I can sing along to has me totally enthralled for days. When I saw the Diet Coke advert, I thought it was gross. All those people drinking the same bottle of Coke and then kissing everyone else who has ever drunk a bottle of Coke. I mean nothing against Diet Coke – which I love – but it just seems icky. Someone tried to explain to me that was not what the advert was saying, but I didn't really get it.

Yours,
Emma Louise Bridge

P.S. Note to self: Stop watching adverts.

COMMENTARY

This diary entry raises an issue that can have serious consequences: the ability to say 'no'.

Both girls have difficulty with this issue and we have had to give them certain phrases to use to help them and prevent being in a situation where they do not know what to say. That is always when the difficulties arise: when they have nothing to say and suddenly have signed up for something or agreed to something they later regret.

The unsolicited telephone calls raising money have caused a lot of problems and at first we had to remove the phone from Emma before she made a wrong decision. We have since taught her phrases to say, but it still remains a challenge we are working on. It relates very much to self-confidence and that is also an area that we are helping Emma with.

KEY POINTS AND ADVICE

• Learn certain phrases to end a conversation, especially when you can't think of anything else to say.

• Practise telephone conversations in a controlled manner, setting tasks such as booking appointments, ringing relatives and so on. The more practice on the phone they have, the more comfortable and confident they will become.

- Write down things to say and have them by the phone to help with the unexpected phone calls.

- Where self-confidence is a problem, work at building up confidence through supported interaction in various situations, modelling and demonstrating how they could react. Gradually withdraw the support as it is no longer needed.

- Avoid over-exposure to things that will cause a problem. You cannot avoid everything but you can limit exposure to adverts, for example.

- Emma has ill-advisedly signed up for charities in the street when in the past she was more able to go out. It is important to encourage openness and communication at home so that you can help to sort things out and cancel any commitments that should not have been undertaken in the first place.

- It may be necessary to monitor bank accounts in a sensitive way in order to check they have not signed up for a good cause they cannot afford. I do not mean underhand checking, but discussing and ensuring the young adult has not got into difficulties in this way.

BEING HOME ALONE

Dear Diary,

I have to be home alone today. I am writing in you early because of that. I suppose everyone has to be home alone at some point. Some probably more than me. I am not home alone all that often. It's fine really.

Wait, got to go check the doors and windows are shut and locked.

Right back. Yes, so I was saying it's not that bad.

Hang on, haven't checked the garden is empty… Right, no signs of burglars. Though while I am thinking about it, I should probably make a note of all the noises I can hear to make sure I know what they all are.

Right, made my list. I cannot hear anything out of the ordinary so I think we are okay. Oh, though should do another list again later. For now it's fine. Oh wait, do I know where they were, when they are getting home and why they are out? Mum did tell me. I should probably write that down somewhere.

Right, made myself a neat little note. Also noted down every possible emergency contact number while I was at it.

Right, now I am fine. I do feel sick and worried but that's normal, right?

Yours,
Emma Louise Bridge

COMMENTARY

Forward planning, detailing what is happening, being able to contact us if needed, checking in to see if she is okay, routine safety checks before we leave and sticking to our schedule where possible are all necessary for trips out when Emma is left alone. This does not happen often, and the anxiety she feels is related to her general state of anxiety which has been heightened by the move. Success leads to success, and starting out with short trips out and ensuring we stick to what we say helps to build her confidence for the next time. Over time we have been able to leave her more.

KEY POINTS AND ADVICE

- Forward planning is essential.

- Be clear about where you are going and how long you will be.

- Provide contact details and check in to see if all is okay.

- We plan ahead what to do if Emma feels anxious – for example, self-calming techniques.

- Start with a short trip out and build up to longer times home alone.

- Be aware that some days are better than others and so coping will be better on some days than others.

- Enlist the support of neighbours and friends if necessary. Knowing that someone is available is sometimes all that is needed.

JUST DON'T

Dear Diary,

Someone told me today that in order to not think in a way that society deems 'weird' you simply need to stop thinking that way. Some people seem to believe the key to changing the way someone thinks is to tell them not to think that way. Of course, if it was that easy to change someone's mind, then no one would argue. Or everyone would argue because everyone would always be changing everyone else's mind and no one would know what they thought. I mean, when I am in a social situation and I think the way someone else is doing something is stupid, I am told not to tell them they are being stupid. So I don't tell them. But no matter how hard I try, I still think they are being stupid.

Also, why do people have no problem informing me when they think I am doing something 'weird' and telling me how I 'should' be doing it? It's like someone held a big worldwide meeting and there was a vote and everyone universally decided that if you have an official diagnosis then you are doing something wrong. Surely my way is not always wrong just because it's different from other people's way? I mean everyone's way is weird to someone.

Everyone has the right to be themselves… except those who really do have stupid ways. For example, you cannot go out and break the law under the premise that everyone's hobbies are weird to someone.

My mum says I can't change other people but I can change my point of view so it doesn't upset me any more. Or at least try to change my point of view.

Yours,
Emma Louise Bridge

P.S. Unless it's breaking a law, like that one that says all taxi cabs are required to carry a bale of hay.

COMMENTARY

In this diary entry three issues seem to be evident. The first is the appropriateness of saying what you think regardless of whether this is socially acceptable or will cause offence to someone. Second is the difficulty of coping with the way other people do things when it just seems wrong and you want to change it. The third is how damaging it is to the confidence of a person with ASD to be told constantly they are 'wrong' and to be made to feel that their way is in some way strange and needs changing.

Emma has struggled with this, but has over time she learned that there are things you say in public and things you don't. It is often more the stress of not saying anything and watching someone do something in a way that seems, in Emma's words, 'stupid' that is difficult. Also, conversely, it is other people being free with their opinion and criticising the way she does something because it is not their way of doing it.

An example of this is when Emma tried some charity work in a shop for a short time. She noticed the hangers holding the clothes were all hooked on one way which in her mind seemed wrong. She had her justification for thinking this – it was more difficult to get at the clothes and unhook from the rack, and it looked wrong.

She spent a long time rearranging the clothes so the hangers were reversed. She was told later to put them all back as the manager wanted them the other way.

Emma still feels this was stupid. She did not say so to the manager, but she was very stressed and struggled to keep calm and carry on her work. When I picked her up, she told me about it with obvious distress.

We talked through the situation, and although she still holds to her view, she accepts that others will not be of the same opinion always and there are times when she has to accept another person's wishes. This was the manager of the shop and so what she said was final. I use other familiar situations and family members to make the point and help to generalise the learning.

This is a process that we repeat in different scenarios, and Emma is learning to cope and respond in a less stressed way.

KEY POINTS AND ADVICE

- Use everyday scenarios and situations to discuss difficulties and work out solutions.

- Allow time to share and listen to what caused the stress and then look at ways of reducing it in future.

- Don't expect a person with ASD to 'change their mind'. Like Emma, though, they can learn to accept why they need to adapt. They may still think they are right – we are all entitled to our opinion – and their opinion is valid, but there are times when other people's opinions are held to be more important, as in the example of the charity shop where the manager is the boss.

- By looking at a variety of situations, learning is more likely to be transferred so it becomes generalised to different situations. This takes time.

- Learning what to say and what not to say in social situations is tricky – if we are honest, many of us struggle. It is refreshing to be totally honest but not to the extent of offending people. Patience, guidance, modelling behaviour, accepting who they are but challenging inappropriate behaviour can be used in a positive way. Suggest alternatives words or phrases rather than just saying 'Don't say that.'

BE QUEEN FOR THE DAY

Dear Diary,

If you cannot stand anything to do with the monarchy – though I can't really comprehend that being possible of anyone – stop reading now because I am in full monarchy mood today. Though this is a diary and my diary would most definitely like the monarchy. So forget that.

I was reading random stuff online today. When you're socially awkward like me, being online always feels better because it's possible without leaving the house. Though leaving the house is good. No one should just stop leaving the house and be online. That's bad.

I am so easily distracted today.

So I saw this pop-up thing saying 'What if you could be queen for the day?' Of course I am not the queen and never could be the queen. So I don't know what I would do if I was the queen because I am not the queen. However, if someday the government decides to host a 'give a random person power' event where they invite a commoner to make rules (or I marry a prince) and I somehow got some power, I do have an idea what it would be cool to do.

I would make sure everything in the entire country had an assigned place. Except for things designed to be transported, but they could still have a 'going home' space. I would make sure every family was given a house and in that house would be a set of stuff all in its pre-assigned place with labels on everything telling people what it is and where it should be. Except the labels would be sticky so if the people wanted to give something a new assigned place they could stick the label somewhere else. Only if they absolutely had to.

I would give everyone in the country their own colour with a little square sticker in the right colour to remind them what it is. Now, you wouldn't have to dress in that colour or anything. That would be boring. No, everyone can dress how they like. The colour is so that everyone would have their stuff either in that colour or with a little sticker in that colour stuck on the item. That way no one could steal stuff because everyone could see if you had stuff in the wrong colour. Also everything would be fair because everyone would have an equal amount in their own individual colour. And I would have a big suggestion box and everyone in the country could write their suggestions on little pieces of paper in their colour. Then I would hire someone who had the sole job of filing the suggestions according to a pre-designed coordinated filing system. Then I would read through them all and answer them.

I am fully aware I have not gone through the realism aspect of this plan, but I think I have time to work out the kinks before the government invent that day I mentioned at the top. Oh, and I don't really have time to explain it all. Free bouncy castles for every child's birthday, a universal spending limit on presents and a worldwide Secret Santa but with a different name like 'fabulous Father Christmas Super Secret Generous Giveaway'. It's a working title. Oh, and definitely bring over that 'emotionally registered companion dogs' system so that people with mental health difficulties over here could use the service. Oh, and something to help those in the forces… Right, should stop now.

Yours,
Emma Louise Bridge

COMMENTARY

Not much to say on this one – Emma allowing her thoughts free rein.

A wonderful imagination has led to her creativity and is very much part of her personality.

PANIC ATTACK THOUGHTS

Dear Diary,

I had a panic attack today. It is seriously icky when I have one. It feels like the world is going to implode. I am hiding out in my room right now to calm down. The sooner I can figure out how to move on from this social anxiety the better. 'Autism is for life – Social Anxiety shouldn't be' or something.

So my thoughts during a panic attack go something like this…

I don't like this. Too many people. Far too many people on the street at the same time. I really don't like this. Why did I leave the house today? Oh yeah, because it's good and healthy and required for living. Can I leave? Well, I am walking home, so not really. Just have to keep walking home. Okay, walk faster. But if I walk faster, then I might trip and fall. Then I might break something and be helpless. Okay, walk slowly and carefully. Right, I am meant to be practising my breathing. I am breathing. Wait – am I breathing? In and out. In and out. Right, yes,

I am breathing. Okay, I am trying to be calm. I am looking around. The world is not scary. The world is fine. Oh look, a wall. That wall has some litter on. Has no one noticed that litter? Shouldn't someone move that litter? There is no bin. Why is there no bin? Where is the bin? There is litter and no bin! What do I do? Oh wait, meant to be walking home. Right, my breathing is slowing. I am walking carefully. I am calming down. I am fine. Except I am not fine. That is a lie. I am panicking. But I am not supposed to be panicking.

Okay, try again… My breathing is supposed to be slowing down. Though that is not what I am supposed to say. She didn't mention using the words 'supposed to' when giving me instructions on breathing through a panic attack. I am supposed to say 'I am breathing slowly'. Except I am not. I am breathing fast. Because I am panicking. Wait – why was I panicking? Because something was scary. But what? I can't remember. Oh no, something is scary and I don't know what it is! It could get me at any time! Help! Wait – I was supposed to be breathing… Ahhh, too many people!

Yours,
Emma Louise Bridge

COMMENTARY

Over the years Emma has suffered from panic attacks in various situations. They can happen at home, when she is out with the family or if she on her own. The panic attacks are related to her social anxiety and events that have happened in her life, but also her autism makes the world a scarier place. We lost our dog a few months ago and she feels a lot less safe since he died.

When she is at home or I am out with her, I talk her through her panic attack, getting her to focus on her breathing. The act of breathing in through the nose and out of the mouth, even counting the breaths, helps to steady her breathing to a slower pace. This does not always help when she is on her own as is evident from her diary entry.

As her breathing slows, I talk to her, keeping her focus away from the perceived threat or stress and on me. If I am aware of what has caused the panic, we seek a solution to the problem, or I find out what is causing it and then seek a solution. It may be removing ourselves from the situation, talking through the issue and finding an acceptable way forward, keeping calm at all times, not making generalised statements but specific ones related to what we are going to do. For example, it is not helpful to say 'Oh, it will be fine'.

If Emma is on her own, she attempts the breathing technique and then employs a variety of other methods to divert her mind away from the perceived threat or stressful situation. She will remove herself from it if possible, contact a family member or sing to herself her favourite children's bible songs to help her focus away from her fears.

From previous therapy she has learned to imagine a 'happy place' in her mind which she can think about and which diverts her thinking away from the feelings of stress.

There are various therapies available but this is not the place to discuss them.

KEY POINTS AND ADVICE

- Focus on slowing the breathing – deeper and slower (unless this causes more stress).

- Count breaths in and out – in through the nose and out through the mouth.

- Emma's happy place is a place in her mind which she can go to – being a shark (a good thing) swimming around. This diverts her thoughts away from the perceived threat.

- When accompanying her, I make direct statements about what we are going to do. Avoid statements like 'You're fine.' It is useful to have direct statements that will counteract the problem, especially when the panic is because something has gone wrong.

- Try to pinpoint the trigger. After the panic has calmed, work through how to deal with future situations. Do not do this too soon.

- I keep her focused on me and away from the perceived threat.

- Have a sensory bag with items that are calming and reduce stress – a stress ball is an example, but items will be individual to the person.

- At the time it may be necessary to withdraw from the situation/stimulus or whatever is causing the problem. Although social anxiety needs to be faced and issues tackled, this should be done in a gradual way and some situations may need to be worked up to before they can be overcome.

- As Emma gains more independence, it is important that she learns to control and deal with any panic attacks herself, using the strategies mentioned above.

- Plan ahead if a trigger is known and can be avoided by forward planning. This isn't often possible as panic attacks can just come on unexpectedly.

- Seek further advice or intervention from a specialist. As I have mentioned before, it is important that this specialist understands the nature of ASD as well as social anxiety and panic attacks.

THINGS PEOPLE SAY

Dear Diary,

Today someone who I used to go to school with messaged me online. I prefer to chat online because there is no tone of voice. That way, if I say something that people would normally take offence at, they assume it's a joke online. Not that I do it on purpose. It just works out that way. Anyway, so I got chatting to this person and the topic of my autism came up. I am pretty open about it because I don't feel it's something to be embarrassed or ashamed about. No more than telling people I have ginger hair or I am short. Though some people would find admitting those two things embarrassing.

So in response they said, 'That is a new thing, huh? I mean, you acquired that after school, right? 'Cos you didn't seem that weird at school. Plus you said you got the diagnosis this year.'

That response made no sense to me. Autism is not a disease. You cannot pick it up like the common cold. You also cannot go into a shop and acquire 'some autism please'. If I did, then I forgot to read the small print saying you can't return it and you have it for life now. Not that I don't want my autism. It's part of me and I don't mind it. More like if I bought it and then found out I got the autism but not a savant gift or anything, I would at least want a refund.

I am sure the person was not trying to insult me. Well, not sure – I can't really tell these things – but probably not. I just didn't understand what they meant. I was born with autism. It is a condition that is diagnosed later in girls but is present from birth. Admittedly, a lot of people don't seem to be aware of this. But the thing is, nothing about me has drastically changed. It is not like I developed symptoms. The way I act is the way I have always acted on the most part, bar my social anxiety getting worse – but that's a whole different issue. Some things are more prominent now, admittedly. However, I didn't wake up one morning and suddenly want to put everything in a certain place and take everything I was told literally… They didn't notice my behaviour, rush me into hospital and diagnose me with 'an unfortunate case of autism'. Getting a diagnosis explains why I act the way I do; it does not make me act the way I do. I didn't get autism the moment I got the diagnosis; I had autism and got a diagnosis.

Yours,
Emma Louise Bridge

COMMENTARY

This is a topic we have already looked at, but Emma and I both felt it was important to reiterate. This diary entry shows up a common misconception about autism and especially about girls and autism. Some think that this is not a condition that affects girls at all, but, as we know, this is not true. Yes, it tends to occur more in boys, but I have two girls with Asperger's syndrome (or ASD as it is now usually called) and in my work with children with autism I have worked with girls, although not many.

As mentioned before, girls often present for diagnosis late as they can be better as young children at mimicking others; they may have imaginary friends and imaginary worlds, and often have only one friend who helps them and gives them guidance. They can show no interest in fashion; for example, Emma's sister went through a phase of wearing only boy's clothes. They may favour more 'boyish' activities, such as those that involve being physically fearless. Emma used to jump off high things and show little sign of fear when she was younger. This 'tomboyish' attitude can be expressed either as fearlessness or as a form of over-the-top physical anger. But it can also be the opposite in that they can intently focus on 'girlish' play in a repetitive way.

In both Emma's and her sister's case, they did not obviously present with ASD in early childhood and nothing was flagged up through school. It was not until their late teens and early 20s that they were assessed and received a diagnosis. Obviously the condition had been there since birth, but it was not identified until later. It was through our insistence as parents that we finally managed to start the process leading to diagnosis.

It is so important that people understand this to prevent the misunderstandings that Emma describes. It is also vital that girls are identified earlier as being on the spectrum so they can receive the support and help they need as they are growing up.

As Emma says, the diagnosis makes sense of her world and it has opened doors to help that would not have been available to her or her sister if they had not received a diagnosis. They do not see it as a negative or a label that diminishes them in some way.

I would say to parents/carers or those working with children to be vigilant, especially with girls, so any signs can be picked up early. Having worked with young children with autism for several years, I know the benefit of early intervention.

KEY POINTS AND ADVICE

- Be aware and informed about the differences between girls and boys on the autistic spectrum or potentially on the spectrum.

- Don't be afraid to request assessment.

- Be open and honest about the issues. When people don't understand, explain.

- We have explained to both the girls why it may have taken so long to gain a diagnosis. When we look back with hindsight, we can see a pattern that at the time was less obvious.

- We have been told that supportive parents 'scaffold' their children in their learning and this can mask the true picture until their child has to start becoming more independent. As parents, we support, encourage and help our children, which is good, but it can have the effect of covering up difficulties which emerge later. This is particularly true if they have other medical problems which need treating and extra support.

- We would encourage looking into diagnosis as it has opened doors to support for the girls that wasn't there before. And as Emma said, it helped her to make more sense of her world and the way she thinks.

• There are many misconceptions about autism when a late diagnosis is made and nothing has apparently been picked up earlier. ASD is from birth but may not present itself until later or be recognised in its full form until young teenage years or young adulthood, especially in girls. I have even read of women in their 50s who have been diagnosed and suddenly things have fallen into place in their minds. It is not a disease and it is not something that suddenly comes on. We have struggled with this when looking back, wondering why had no one picked up or noticed anything, but it doesn't mean the signs were not there – just that they were well hidden until later in development. Hindsight is a marvellous thing, and although we helped, adapted and put in place support for our children, as all parents do, it was hard when they had difficulties to put the pieces of the puzzle together and see the whole picture. As I started working with children with autism and as the autistic traits became more marked, it became more evident to us and eventually to others and a diagnosis was made. Many people do not realise this and that is where misunderstanding occurs and comments can be made.

IMPOSSIBLY
CONFUSING

Dear Diary,

I wish someone would show me this book on society's rules. All these unspoken rules everyone seems to know that I don't have any clue about and that tell you how to act. If no one will show me this book, I am going to write one about all the rules I have learned thus far. Talking about rules, I was listening to the news today and they were talking about being politically correct. What people can and cannot say. I am always trying to learn what I am allowed to say and what I am not.

For example:

'Your idea is stupid' – cannot say.

'Can we try it a different way?' – can say.

It reminded me of this quote I saw online saying 'Autism is just a label people use as an excuse for being rude.' According to the rules of political correctness, no one is allowed to be rude. Well, that seems weird because I work really hard on trying to learn what I am allowed to say, and so if I wanted an excuse to be rude, why would I bother?

It all makes no sense to me. Plus no one seems to have defined the rules on what's rude. How come if I say to someone 'I think the way you're doing that is stupid' it's rude, but someone can say to me something like 'You can't do that, autistic people can't do that and you're autistic' and it's not rude? How come if I say to someone of Asian descent 'Do you know my dad? He was born in Hong Kong' it's taken as rude because being Asian doesn't mean you know every other person connected to Asia? However, someone thinks it's perfectly okay to say to me 'Oh my friend's/ neighbour's/second cousin's child had autism – perhaps you know them?' Like there is some big register of names listed somewhere so I can keep track and make sure I am acquainted with everyone with the same diagnosis.

(I would love it if there was a big register of names listed somewhere.)

I mean, maybe some people do think those things are rude and wouldn't say them. But then how do you know whether it's a rule or not? It's so confusing.

Other things I just don't understand why the person saying them didn't feel they were rude:

- 'You don't look autistic.'

- 'You can't be autistic because [fill in variety of reasons].'

- 'Are you like Rain Man?'

- 'You're autistic? Does that mean you're backward?'

- 'You're too intelligent to be autistic.'

- 'I know an autistic person, and you don't act like he or she does.'

- 'This child I know had autism, but they put him on a special diet and he got better.'

- 'You can get over it. It's just in your head. It's not physical.'

- 'No one would even know you have autism – you must be so proud of yourself.'

I think the worst one out of all of those is 'he got better'. I am not sick and I cannot 'get better' and I don't want to 'get better'. I want to fit into society and be accepted, but I don't want to completely remove what makes me me for the sake of making society happy.

Yours,
Emma Louise Bridge

P.S. Sorry about the rant. I know lots of awesome
people who are so accepting and nice.

COMMENTARY

This one stands alone without comment from me.

DOING A TALK

Dear Diary,

Today I was clearing out space on my computer. While going through the documents and deciding what to keep, I found a speech I had given in school in front of a bunch of people on 'Why summer stinks?' The teacher wanted us to have topics we would find difficult. Actually, I found writing the topic pretty easy. Snowmen die, everyone is sweaty and icky, sunburn is a health hazard and I have to put my collection of boots away till winter. However, giving the talk was less easy. Admittedly, I find standing in front of a room full of people and giving a talk makes me feel marginally less scared than holding a coherent conversation with someone one-on-one sometimes. Or even being in the audience at an event and surrounded by people. At least on the stage or at the front of the classroom you are not surrounded by people. I hate being surrounded by people. But back to the talk. Giving a talk is still pretty high up on the list of scary things.

I remember after this particular talk people told me I was 'so calm' and I must have found it 'so easy'. Now, I confess I do love talking about myself and could do so for hours. I also love talking about topics I have any knowledge on. Oh, and helping people. So if I have something to say that could help people, that is awesome. However – find it easy? Yeah, my thoughts at the time went something like this.

Okay, so I am giving a talk. It is fine. I have it written down. Just read the script. But then they won't see my face. Do they need to see my face? Well, the teacher said to look at the audience. But then I can't see my script! Look up. Look down. Look up. Look down. Okay, right, maybe I can picture something not scary. Someone told me once to imagine the audience naked. Okay, but why is this less scary? I am in a room full of naked people! Am I naked? No, I am not naked. Except, why are they all naked and I am not? Should I be? Is this a dream? Usually in a dream it would be me naked. Not everyone else naked. But then in reality people don't walk around naked.

No, wait – talk. Right, trying to give talk. What about imagining no one is listening and I am talking to myself. Okay, I am just reading the talk out to myself. Right, this is all right. This isn't awful. Wait – did someone just cough? Were they coughing because they have a bad throat? Is someone getting them some water? No one is getting them water! They must have been coughing to tell me that I am going on too long! But I have two pages left… What can I skip out? Oh wait, maybe it was a cough to say I am being rude. Which bit was rude? Tell me, random stranger! Tell me! Oh gosh, I feel sick… How was I rude? Okay, I will just move on. Wait – I've lost my place. Where am I? Oh gosh, I need to sit down. Oh wait – I reached the end of the talk… Well, that was all right.

Yours,
Emma Louise Bridge

COMMENTARY

Emma has always struggled with doing anything in front of people, especially giving talks. We found in the end the only way to help her with this was to ensure her preparation was done well and then she practised in front of us on several occasions until she was confident that she knew her subject well. Her confidence varies depending on her general anxiety level, but preparation and practice have helped.

KEY POINTS AND ADVICE

- Planning ahead is essential.

- Practise multiple times in front of family or friends.

- Knowing the subject really well is important.

- Using relaxation techniques beforehand can be helpful.

- Use a larger font and more spacing for the text so there is no strain in trying to read it.

- If there are options of doing the talk in front of a smaller audience, this may be a possibility.

- Be available to talk through things as near to the event as possible, especially if panicking is likely.

- Use a stress ball or other stress reliever if necessary.

GOOD GIRL

Dear Diary,

Mum told me I was a good girl this morning. I had done the dishes in the sink and then gone to her to receive affirmation I had done the right thing. When you have difficulties, in my case autism and social anxiety, people are very good at telling you all the ways you could be doing better. Go up to anyone and ask, and it seems they can list off the top of their head all the way you don't do things right, you don't fit in, you act 'weird'.

I guess it's probably because of this that I love being told 'good girl' or 'yes, that was a good job' or 'well done'. I suppose I like to celebrate the little things. Today I made a phone call and did not have a panic attack. To me that is a big deal. Somehow when you make a big deal about the little things, it makes the world seem a bit happier. I mean celebrating little achievements like not making big problems out of little problems. That does not make the world happy. That makes the world stressful. A stressful world is a sad one – trust me, I know.

No one should make your world all about what you can't do. So I have decided to try to tell myself I am a 'good girl' every morning. Okay, it might sound a bit like I am a dog. But, honestly, dogs that hear 'good girl or boy' in the right tone of voice are usually happy about it. Well, 'good girl' or 'good boy'. If they heard 'good girl or boy', they would think you didn't care enough to work out their gender. Or they wouldn't, because I don't know what dogs think. Maybe the key to being happy is to let the little things make you happy… I don't know.

Other people don't seem as easily amused by things as me. I can be entertained for ages by flashing lights, shiny things, anything that is fluffy, things you can fiddle with without breaking, anything that is squishy without being icky…the list goes on.

Yours,
Emma Louise Bridge

COMMENTARY

Emma flags up how important it is to focus on the positive and not the negative. It is so easy to try to 'help' by saying 'This is the way you should do this' or 'You could have done it that way', but this can be so negative. As Emma says, celebrating the little achievements, setting up situations for their success, means that confidence will grow and lead to more success. I find I need to notice even the smallest things and ensure I encourage and praise the girls. This is especially true when they have tried to do something I have suggested and then I notice something else needs doing instead of recognising their achievement. It is a learning curve for all of us. We all need encouragement – some more than others – especially when life is a struggle and confusing a lot of the time.

KEY POINTS AND ADVICE

- Notice the little things and give praise.

- Try to focus on the positive and not the negative.

- Small steps for some are big steps forward for others.

- Set up situations for success as this leads to more success.

- We still find rewards are a big incentive, even if they are rather more expensive than they used to be.

- Be careful to be fair between siblings.

- Rewards charts give a visual picture of achievements and can be personalised to the individual. Even young adults can still enjoy this type of visual system. They can develop their own with pictures of favourite characters, film stars, collectables, etc.

IN SHOPS

Dear Diary,

You might want to prepare yourself for today's entry. Is that enough preparation time? There was a packet of shrimp in the vegetable section of the shop today. Bet you weren't prepared for something that bad. It was just sitting there all in the wrong section. It should have been in the fridge section. It was a fridge product. I went and told the sales person it was in the wrong place. She didn't move it, though. Normally, I would move it myself. But I couldn't put it back because I don't know how long it had been out of the fridge and it might have been off. So I tried to just forget about it, but it was so hard.

Then later on there was a bag of prawn crackers in the chocolate aisle. Prawn crackers are not even remotely like chocolate. I like both foods, but in their own assigned section. I put them in my trolley. Mum likes it when I try not to tidy because otherwise we would be in the shop for hours. It's good for me to try to leave a shop without having been hours. So putting them in my trolley was not tidying them but it was removing them from the wrong section.

In the sauce aisle, someone had put some tomato pasta sauce in the wrong sauce section. The tomato section is right next door. It would have taken two steps to get to the right section. I just don't understand why someone would put something in the wrong section and then just walk away? As though everything is fine. Knowing that thing is in the wrong section. Knowing they are solely responsible for that thing being in the wrong section. I think the only excuse for this is if your child picks something up and you don't want to buy it and you're stressed and trying to contain small children and shop.

For all those who don't have small children... I don't understand it!

I really wish I could get a job in one of these shops just putting things in the right place all day. I would just organise and tidy to my heart's content. If my social anxiety didn't prevent it at the moment and if the job existed, that would be awesome.

Yours,
Emma Louise Bridge

COMMENTARY

Shopping is an interesting experience in our household. Both my girls hate seeing things in the wrong place and both have very strong urges to put all items back where they should be, which, as you can imagine, is impractical and would mean our shopping trips would take hours.

In order to help with this problem, we have devised a system where I allow them to return a certain number of items to their right place per trip. Obviously, the fridge item could not be returned and so Emma passed the information on to a sales assistant.

I have found that by gradually challenging them on this behaviour we have managed to arrive at a compromise which makes the shopping trip a suitable length but allows them to fulfil the strong urge to tidy up. I allow a certain amount of tidying at the checkout of small items while we wait, but only while we are paying.

KEY POINTS AND ADVICE

• Make a plan and stick to it.

• Allow a certain amount of the obsessive behaviour and then no more. If this is arranged beforehand and agreed upon, then everyone knows what is going to happen.

USING THE PHONE /
HAVING A SCRIPT

Dear Diary,

I had to use the phone today. I wish everyone in the world had a script. So I would know exactly what they were going to say and I would have all the exact decided answers. I wish this in all conversations but mostly in phone ones. I write down what I am going to say, but people never say the right thing back. I like writing. I could write everyone scripts. Then everyone would know everything that was going to be said.

I do not like the phone at all. Nowadays I can use it more than when I used to refuse to. However, I still find it highly stressful. You have to get the number you're ringing right. You don't know you didn't get it wrong till someone answers and then you have to deal with that if you have. You have to hope the right person answers even if you got the right number. Then you have to say the right thing. Knowing the whole time they could say anything at all. Plus you don't want to leave them waiting so you don't have thinking time. Emails give you time to think. Oh, and time to go ask advice. Plus you can't undo stuff you have said on the phone. Even if the person didn't hear you say it. I know I have said it and that is the same.

Plus the phone makes me feel stupid because I get all panicky when I have to press buttons for options. There is never an option that exactly covers what I want. Oh, and I can never recognise anyone's voice on the phone. Everyone sounds the same. I can sometimes tell gender but that's it. I always have to talk myself into it when I need to use the phone. Some days this takes longer than others. Though it does always make me smile when I put the phone down because I know it's over, at least until the next phone call.

The other reason why the phone is awful is that everyone always wants to know your mobile number on every form, even though I really want them to ring my home number because I hate the mobile even more than the landline. I can never hang up on people. Not even automated voices or sales people. I have been told so many times to hang up on sales people, but I can't do it. I lose count of the number of questionnaires I have done and had to answer half the questions 'no idea' because I didn't want to be rude but didn't know the stuff they wanted to know. I can't hang up on automated voices because it might be a person. Plus the voice belonged to a person once.

Yours,
Emma Louise Bridge

COMMENTARY

Phone calls produce a challenge, as Emma has described. It has been a difficult task that both girls have faced, and we have worked with them so that they are able to make and receive calls successfully. I cannot say they like it or want to do it, but I can say that they are able. They started off refusing to use the phone at all, and when they did, often it would be put down if the conversation got difficult and I would have to pick up the remainder of the call and sort things out with the caller. It was often easier to make a call myself than insist they did it themselves, but obviously this was not helping their independence.

Setting challenges – starting small and building up – has enabled them to achieve. I started by sitting near and the call would be planned, information written down that was to be imparted and extra information that may be needed, and I could assist if needed during the call. They developed this skill to the point of not needing me near, although I still find I am needed on some occasions, especially with calls relating financial or medical matters.

I have to admit that the phone is still not a method of communication they would choose to use, but at least now they are capable of doing so.

KEY POINTS AND ADVICE

- Plan ahead and write down what they are going to say and why they are ringing.

- Arrange set tasks that need to be completed, starting small and building on success.

- Make using the phone meaningful, not just for the sake of it.

- Be on hand to assist if necessary at first, withdrawing as confidence grows.

- Many of us do not like using the phone – they may never like it – but it is the skill of being able to do so that matters.

- Answering the phone is a more challenging process as it is less in the control of the person with ASD and they do not know who is at the other end or what they will say.

- If necessary, teach polite phrases to answer the phone and how to elicit the information needed to see who the call is for.

- It may be easier to do it for them, but it is important to build independence through overcoming these difficulties. Certainly the girls now are better on the phone, although answering it is still an issue with no one rushing to pick it up in our house.

• Social communication groups are useful in addressing issues like this. Within the group setting, challenges are set for during the week and then reported back on the following week.

• For answerphone messages, be prepared with a written message which can be read out if the person called is not available and they need to leave a message.

HOLIDAYS

Dear Diary,

I am on holiday at the moment. Well, actually I am on a retreat for a week to help with my issues. I won't go into the details, but it means I am writing to you from somewhere that is not home. I bet that makes a nice change for you. Mum drove me and we got lost. We took a wrong turning somewhere and then things got all confusing. It was pitch-black by the end of the journey and the whole time it was foggy. I was feeling rather fragile by the time we arrived because I hate the dark, being outside in the dark, getting lost, being late (which we were by the time we arrived) and being anywhere without someone I know. I think it was perfectly reasonable that when my mum left I cried. Everyone seems very nice…but I don't know them.

Ugh, I am going to go to bed…

Dear Diary,

Sorry I didn't come back, Diary. Now it's the next day already. I didn't sleep last night and so felt like taking one of my bedtime pals with me to breakfast. You will know about my bedtime pals from a previous entry. I resisted because my room has two beds and just me staying in it, and so I had tucked my two bedtime pals into the other bed and they looked too cosy to move. So instead I focused on getting there exactly for when breakfast started. Found a chair with its back to the wall exactly how I like. Always safer in a chair with your back to the wall. Had two slices of the gluten-free bread, covered in butter to try to help the bits go down – note to self: it was actually very nice and you couldn't even taste the bits with enough butter on – and tried not to think about the fact everyone was talking and it was loud and… Right, need to stop writing that before I freak myself out again. Are you getting spooked just thinking about it? No? Well, then you probably don't have issues like mine – good for you. But then you are a diary and are relatively issue-free in general, presumably.

Nothing really was a problem until my favourite time of the day came – any part of the day where food is being served, but in this case dinner. However, eating dinner is always highly complex for me. Basically, a combination of food allergies, inability to eat certain textures due to my autism and the personal preferences that everyone has makes it remarkably hard to explain to someone what I can and cannot eat. To make things simple, famous last words, I told the chef I was vegetarian, gluten-free and couldn't eat tomatoes. The last two are food allergies and the first is because there is so much meat I just cannot stand the taste of. I didn't want to mention that I also cannot eat food with bits in due to my texture issues and cannot eat spicy food due to my hypersensitivity.

Keep all that in mind, Diary. So dinner arrives and it's chicken curry. The nice lady handing it out tells me to just push the chicken off because there has been a mix-up and someone else has my vegetarian dish. Now, I really don't mind doing this. Except I take one bite of the food and it feels like my mouth is burning. Seriously, four glasses of water later and I still felt uncomfortable. I didn't want to complain, because I am incapable of doing so or saying no to people, so I just looked down at my plate, waiting for someone to notice. One of the ladies on the table offered to get me a cheese sandwich. A gluten-free cheese sandwich, of course. So when it arrives, I notice it's that gluten-free bread that is filled with bits. Now I am in rather a big dilemma. They have gone and got me something special and it was so sweet of them…but I cannot stand bits. I just cannot eat food with bits. Panicking a bit, I cut off the crusts, smooshed the middle together and, focusing on the nice cheese and butter middle, ate it as best I could. When asked if I was enjoying it, I said yes, because I was thinking of the cheese and butter part.

Feeling rather proud of myself, I waited for dessert. Once again they had done me something specially gluten-free. It was raspberries, cream and some coconut thing. Now once again…you have guessed it, I just cannot stand the taste of coconut. The thing is I cannot help it. I really don't want to be a bother, though. So, feeling guilty, I cut the cake into little bits, covered each bit with cream and ate up. After the meal one of the really nice ladies suggested I go see if there were any gluten-free biscuits left. Apparently, they were nice… and ginger. Ginger, as far as I am concerned, goes on the no-spicy-foods-please-don't-make-me-eat-it list. Anyway, I could not really tell the lady no – see my other entry on saying no – and so I just kind of nodded as I always do when faced with a situation I have no idea how to deal with. Another lady hears we are looking for gluten-free cake or biscuits and says they have been put away, but she will go find some in the kitchen. She asks me which I want – cake or biscuits – and, feeling entirely helpless, I respond 'I don't know' because it wasn't me that wanted anything to start with.

The upshot of it is that I have a plate with a ginger biscuit I can't eat, another of the coconut things but now without any cream to aid covering the taste and a rather nice gluten-free Battenburg cake thingy. I did eat that last one and it was delicious. The other two are still sitting on a plate on my bedside table while I try to work out what to do with them. Ah well, time to prepare myself for tomorrow.

Yours,
Emma Louise Bridge

COMMENTARY

This is a very broad topic and I do not even begin to cover it. These are just some of the things that have been issues in our family and I am aware there are so many more that we do not face. Taste, texture, colour, temperature, hypersensitivity to spice, sweet, sour and many other issues can impinge on meal times and make them a very difficult experience for the autistic person and their family. We also have our likes and dislikes, even down to particular brands of foods that we prefer to the exclusion of others. These can also change from one day to another.

The other issues related are food allergies to gluten and wheat, dairy products and a host of other products too many to list. The first two are the ones common in our family.

I am aware from my work with children on the autistic spectrum how eating and mealtimes can be extremely challenging. But wherever you are on the spectrum, the challenges are real and life-affecting, and how we try to work through them as a family may not be helpful to some but may be to others.

When she was younger, Emma appeared to be fussy eater, but as we understood her needs more in relation to the autism, we were able to cater better for her and adapt to make eating and food a more pleasurable experience.

At home it is easier to cater for her and her sister's needs, taking into account texture (e.g. having white bread with no seeds in it), simple plain meals with no spicy food, limiting the amount of meat (she does eat some meat but not chunks or large pieces), gluten-free (which runs in the family anyway) – even the number of items where possible (e.g. fishcakes as discussed in an earlier entry), her own plate, knife, fork, spoon and so on.

Emma has learned to compromise over time by gradually adding in items that she doesn't normally tolerate until they become acceptable. An example of this is the seeded breaded that she accepted with lots of butter when she was away. She would not choose to have this at home but she was able to accept it in this social situation and eat it. She keeps things consistent at home, such as her own plate, but accepts that this is not possible when out and so she uses alternatives for that time only.

Forward planning, ensuring restaurants know our needs prior to arriving, booking a table with seats backing to the wall are all things we do to reduce stress levels and increase enjoyment of the experience. It also helps to go out at quieter times when there are fewer people.

In the situation Emma describes, we had planned ahead but there had been confusion in the arrangements. After that day the food was fine and

Emma had no more problems, except the seeded breaded but she learned to cope with that.

We had several phone calls to discuss what to do with unwanted food and I helped with strategies to ask and ensure that the problems did not repeat themselves. The staff were very supportive and, as they were aware of Emma's needs, they could provide support in general ways by sitting with her, accompanying her from her room to where she needed to be and checking she was okay.

KEY POINTS AND ADVICE

• Food intolerances need to be investigated and may develop or change over time. We have found this within our family and have had to adapt our eating to accommodate. When we go out, we tend to take things with us so we do not have to worry about availability.

• Any eating out or away has to be organised and planned ahead. Ring to check on dietary requirements, check the menu for food that is suitable (no spicy food in our case), arrange for a suitable table and book at a quieter time to minimise the noise levels.

• People are usually helpful when asked, and it is important to prepare the way ahead if a successful trip is going to happen.

- At home we have adapted to the various likes and dislikes and particular needs of the family, and by involving them in the shopping and cooking and listening to their input, situations can be avoided where they are given food they cannot tolerate. We have learned as we go along.

- The main areas we have found difficult with food are spice (even mild), texture (especially bits and lumps), large pieces of meat, sour taste, keeping food separate on the plate, eating in a particular order, dishes with a mixture of foods.

- It is important to explain what 'I can't eat spicy food' really means, for example; people assume it is just a whim and not something that causes distress and is intolerable.

- We have, over time, challenged the girls and gradually introduced items that they would not have tolerated before – for example, we have increased the number of vegetables in a casserole, and Emma also now tolerates more meat than she did – to increase the variety in their diet and develop their ability to be more flexible, but some things remain unchanged.

- We have managed through negotiation to have an arrangement that at home they have the same tableware but when out, as it is a one-off, they cope with what is offered. Home is secure and needs to be the same and so they continue to use the same items at home. When living with a host family, our other daughter did take her plate and bowl with her as she was living there.

• When working in a primary school, we used visual reward charts to encourage children with ASD to sample new foods. We always tried to make it achievable, using small steps, one item at a time and making it fun. It is also a good idea to use the child's particular area of interest as a reward for sampling a new taste or texture. We also looked at the environment in which the children were eating to see if that could be improved to reduce distractions, lower noise levels and make mealtimes a more pleasurable experience which would encourage them to eat.

• Involving children in the whole food process (although this may be difficult if they struggle with handling food or getting their hands dirty) is also a way of encouraging them to try more.

• Although very difficult, it is important to not let it become a battle.

• Set rules and try to keep them.

• Celebrate small steps forward.

LITERAL THINKING

Dear Diary,

Today a lovely nurse put me on some antibiotics for a problem I have with my ears. It said on the instructions to take with water, except I cannot stand water by itself. I was told that you could add a little juice to the water and it would make it okay, but it doesn't say on the leaflet you are allowed to do that. It drives me crazy when leaflets and instructions don't cover everything. Mum did point out to me that they can't cover every tiny eventuality for autistic people who take things too literally. Personally, I don't see why they couldn't put 'take with water unless you hate water in which case take with a water equivalent such as water with juice in' on the label.

It's not the first time that literal thinking has caused a problem in our house. When Mum asks one of us to do a job, such as hoover the upstairs, we won't think to do anything more than exactly the job she has asked us to do. Mum is remarkably patient about it, but you do here her saying 'Why do I live in a house of literal thinkers?' to herself sometimes.

In fact, a few weeks ago I did the shopping for Mum. Well, she had to come with me to the shop and be around to make sure nothing bad happened and write me a super-specific list. But I still sort of did the shopping. Anyway, the literal thing became a real problem when Mum was looking through my trolley.

For example, '1 box of lemon slices' was on the list so I got one box of lemon slices. However, the lemon slices were on offer and usually Mum stocks up on products that are on offer before the offer ends. But Mum does this – she said nothing about me doing it. I had been asked for '1 box of lemon slices' and that was all I was getting.

Yours,
Emma Louise Bridge

COMMENTARY

Life in a literal household can be quite a challenge, as Emma has said. The lemon slices were on offer and I would have expected her to either pick up a few boxes or ask if I wanted more. I should not have expected any more than what she did because she did as I asked, no more, no less, yet I still found myself wondering why she had not done the former.

KEY POINTS AND ADVICE

- If someone has a literal mind, expect them to take you literally and only do exactly what you have asked and no more.

- Have patience and try not to get frustrated: they are not being difficult.

- Give more options or be more specific if more is required.

- I do explain what I would have expected and what they could have done in the circumstances (this happens in a variety of situations) and I find sometimes that they surprise me and pick up on the unsaid expectation.

- Literal thinking comes into all areas of life, and transferring understanding and skills learned from one situation to another may take a long time. It can be very much part of the way a person with ASD thinks. It is important to understand this and it will help to reduce frustration, lower expectations and prevent misunderstandings.

CONSEQUENCES

Dear Diary,

I love getting ready for Christmas. Putting aside the super-stressful art of present giving that I mentioned in an earlier entry. I love the rest of Christmas. Decorating the tree. Wanting an Advent calendar but never remembering to open the little doors. Trying to make everything exactly how it was the year before so everything's nice and routine and involves no change. Though that is not going to be possible this year due to the move. So will have to try and be okay with change this Christmas. Mum and Dad have always made Christmas special for us. We had a chocolate fairy who, if you said a special rhyme to the Christmas tree, would leave chocolate behind. I liked it because the poem was neat and rhymed and the fairy liked the same thing every time which was cool.

When I was little, there was this one Christmas where we had slightly less presents than we usually do. Honestly, Mum and Dad have never let us go short. We have a lot more than a lot of children.

Though I hate it when Mum uses examples of those less fortunate than us to make a point.

Anyway, I looked at the presents and thought 'That is not very much' – so that is exactly what I said. Mum and Dad were really cross and took all my presents away (though they did return them later). At the time I didn't understand what the problem was. I didn't think it was very much. I hadn't been meaning to upset anyone. I was just stating exactly what I thought. I didn't have my autism diagnosis at the time, but now Mum looks back she says it explains why I never really did understand why I got in trouble.

The problem is I have never found it easy to foresee the consequences of things. What will happen after I have said or acted a certain way never tends to occur to me. This is how I end up accidentally offending people or causing arguments. I just say what I think and don't understand that someone else might not see it the way that I see it. I just don't know how to force myself to see the end result that I can't imagine most of the time.

It is not just in things I say, though, that consequences or alternative options seem to elude me. For example, when my brother and I were watching a film last night, the film came to an end but the credits had funny scenes playing to one side while they ran. My brother carried on sitting down.

so it occurred to me afterwards he might have been watching the scenes. However, at the time my thought process was relatively simple. I turned the DVD off because I was done. I took the DVD out of the drive and put it back in its case took it upstairs and put it away in its assigned place on my shelf. Not once during this process did I think that my brother might want to finish watching. It might be he didn't. The point was I didn't think that he could possibly have any other thought process that differed from my own.

Yours,
Emma Louise Bridge

COMMENTARY

The incident with the presents, though we did not understand it at the time, with hindsight showed us a little of how Emma thinks and how we as parents should have reacted differently. Emma did get her presents but not without the upset that could have been avoided. Over time we have noticed that Emma tends to say what she thinks without considering the consequences; if challenged, she often does not realise why what she has said or done could be seen as offensive. This does not mean that we do not challenge her, but it is done with the knowledge based on our understanding of the way she thinks. I do have to act as an intermediary between siblings on occasions where difficulties and misunderstandings arise, explaining why Emma and her sister may say or do things that appear rude or insensitive.

KEY POINTS AND ADVICE

- Be patient and try to understand that they are not being deliberately rude or difficult.

- Be prepared to explain and smooth out misunderstandings with siblings or others.

- Emma's sister carries an autism alert card which she can use in circumstances when she feels it would help for people to know the difficulties she has and to reduce misunderstandings.

- Be prepared to gently challenge and point out when situations arise. We have found this has helped to improve their understanding.

- One of the girls attended a social communications group run by speech therapists, which was very helpful. It was through this that she received the autism alert card, which is also available via the National Autistic Society.

DECISION-MAKING
AND PATTERNS

Dear Diary,

We were out shopping today and as part of the trip we stopped in a material shop on the way home. My blinds had broken and I needed a piece of material to hang up to cover the window. I cannot sleep at night without something there because the big black space freaks me out. Plus the material provides a barrier between me and the outside world. The same as when you hide under your blanket if you hear a scary noise at night. Ineffective perhaps, but something between you and the outside world. The shop was massive. A warren of different passageways between loads of rolls of material. Not good for someone with autism who finds decisions close to impossible to make.

The guy behind the counter was wonderfully patient with me. He found a piece of material that had sunflowers on that he thought would work. However, in order for it to fit my window it had to be on its side. This was a problem because the sunflowers would be pointing sideways. I couldn't have sideways-pointing sunflowers. The stalks have to go down. So that was no good. We considered plain pieces of material, but I wanted something pretty. Well, something pretty and affordable that also matched my room. The guy said to look around and pick because most anything would work for our purposes. But with everything we looked at something was wrong.

The cute owl print one had owls in sunglasses. But half the owls were hanging upside down. Apparently, owls do hang upside down but owls in sunglasses don't hang upside down because how would they keep the sunglasses on? Of course, owls do not wear sunglasses because they do not have ears. The owls in the pictures had pointy tufty bits like some owls do. So you could maybe have balanced sunglasses on those. However, they definitely couldn't have kept the sunglasses on upside down.

Then when I was starting to feel it was hopeless, the store guy suggested some Wallace and Gromit ones he had. We went and found it and it was awesome. The pattern all went in the same direction. It had sheep on, which I love. It was amazing. Only he measured it and it wasn't long enough for my window. We went back to looking, but once I had seen that Wallace and

Gromit material, I knew I had to have it. I have an obsessional personality, as mentioned before, as well as inability to make decisions. I wanted that material so much. I was close to tears. The store guy was great and found a way to cut it so it covered most of my window and the remaining non-broken blinds would cover the rest. It's now up and I am happy. But it just reminds me how hard shopping is. Also how hard decision-making is. I really wish sometimes that I didn't get so upset or annoyed by things. However, that's me and I have to find ways around it somehow. At least it highlights how there are people out there in the world willing to make an effort to accommodate those with issues, and I love little reminders like that.

Yours,
Emma Louise Bridge

COMMENTARY

The blind situation arose because we are in rented accommodation and this was a temporary measure to replace blinds that were broken and which we could not replace ourselves.

Emma had a problem in the material shop because she suffered sensory overload from all the colours, patterns and too much choice. Eventually, when she was offered something and then thought it wasn't possible, it was too much for her. The element of uniformity or lack of it in the pattern on the materials also made it difficult for her as well. The shopkeeper was very patient, which was helpful, and he seemed to understand even though Emma did not tell him (she is often more open when in stressful circumstances).

KEY POINTS AND ADVICE

> Be aware of places that may provide sensory overload so they can be avoided or prepared for.

> Leave it to your older child/young adult to inform people if they wish to share their diagnosis.

> The patience of the shopkeeper was very positive for Emma. It helped her to know that there are people out there who understand and can be accommodating.

- Reduce the number of choices available so that there is not a sensory overload and it is easier to make a decision.

- To avoid upset, try to ensure that something is suitable before offering it.

- Accept what seems to be unusual or strange (such as Emma's views on the patterns on the material) and work within these stipulations as they cannot be changed.

- It may be necessary to leave and return another day or try another shop if the stress levels become too high.

- Do not try to force a choice or this will just make the situation worse.

- Prepare ahead to avoid the situation in the first place.

FRIENDSHIP

Dear Diary,

Today I was going through some old notes for an emotions diary I use to keep. It was an idea suggested by a previous therapist. I had written in the margin of one of the pages: 'I don't need friends.' That had come from the idea the therapist had suggested that some people don't need friends. They manage fine without. Especially those who have a problem connecting with people and forming attachments. I can form attachments. I have people I am very attached to. I struggle doing it because of how hard I find interacting with people sometimes. When the idea was first suggested, I thought it was a great one. I wouldn't have to worry about fitting in or understanding the world or caring about others. I would just have no friends.

However, as time passed I realised it wasn't a solution at all. First, it occurred to me that people who don't have any friends don't get any birthday or Christmas presents. I mean, I have my family but they are not going to be around for ever. My parents will go before me most likely and my siblings will move on and have their own families. If I never made friends and by extension never met anyone either, then no one would be around to give me presents. But putting aside that very important point, I found I just didn't like the idea. I might struggle to understand people and connect with people sometimes, but I don't want to be alone either. I mean, if I ended up alone, I would have to file tax reports…budget my bills… cope with a panic attack without crying and rocking in the corner without any help – the mere idea is terrifying.

I use to find making friends slightly easier. I had friends in infant school. I was a little obsessive and use to find it easiest to focus entirely on one friend. However, as I moved through school, I was bullied badly. My social anxiety got worse. My ability to make friends got worse and worse. The thing is, the autism made understanding other people difficult. The social anxiety made me too scared to try. But I have been told when I am relaxed and happy, I can be quite fun to be around. I suppose I have learned real friends don't mind if you have a shark hat that looks like it's eating your head (as long as you don't wear it all the time) or a collection of Disney DVDs, despite being in your 20s. I have one good online friend and she never minds what I say or do.

She is amazing like that. So I really do hope that I can find friends like that who I can see in the real world. Friends who don't care if I understand them or they understand me but who like me anyway.

Now, if I could only deal with the social anxiety…

Yours,
Emma Louise Bridge

COMMENTARY

Emma has a close relationship with her immediate family. She has also had close friendships in the past which she has enjoyed. Prolonged bullying at school, leading to depression and severe social anxiety, caused a lot of difficulties for her, and she struggled with friendships and social interaction more as she grew older. Also, as the ASD became more evident, leading eventually to her diagnosis, we could look back and see where that had caused issues with friendships and social interaction. Despite this, Emma had always expressed a desire for friends and did not like the thought of being alone. I mention the above because I feel it is important to understand the whole picture in someone's life and not make assumptions because they have a diagnosis of ASD that they will think and feel in a certain way. There are many reasons why Emma struggled and we had to look at all the threads and try to untangle them so they could be addressed in an appropriate way. It is also important not to take things at face value; if someone finds it very hard to interact and communicate socially, it does not mean that they will not be able to or that they do not wish to.

One therapy session Emma attended, which she describes above, highlights where misunderstandings can occur. Emma came from the session feeling she didn't need any friends and would be happy alone – something she had always been worried about being if anything happened to her family. The logic seemed to make sense to her: it would remove all the stresses of social interaction and there would be no need to worry about anyone else or about saying or doing the wrong thing. But she was not happy. After the session. Emma shared with me what they talked about, I listened, we discussed how she felt and I tried to explain the negatives of having no friends (to even out the discussion) and tried to help her explore her feelings. She describes how she felt in her diary entry.

The social anxiety has been a condition that Emma has struggled with for years. Through some therapy, including cognitive behaviour therapy (CBT), and support at home, we are working to build up her confidence, challenging her fears and increasing her ability in social situations. Although social anxiety can be part of ASD, Emma also has social anxiety due to life circumstances and this needs to be addressed in different ways. By helping Emma to build up her confidence in social situations and communication skills and by building her self-esteem, she is more able to meet and make friends, which is important to her. She is very sociable and talkative but finds the demands of close relationships challenging.

KEY POINTS AND ADVICE

- Depression and social anxiety can be linked to ASD but they can also be caused by other situations/events in life. It is important to find out the underlying causes so that the right support and help can be given.

- We have been advised – and through personal experience we have seen for ourselves – how important it is when having therapy that the therapist has an understanding of ASD in order to avoid misunderstandings and to prevent therapy causing more stress than it is meant to relieve. This can be particularly true in the case of CBT (often used in the treatment of social anxiety and depression) where the therapist needs to have a good knowledge of ASD and how a person on the autistic spectrum may think or feel and the extra challenges they face.

- Following any therapy session, Emma and I had time specially put aside to talk and allow Emma to express her feeling or worries and to discuss anything she had not understood during the session. She needed time to work through things.

- We work with Emma on social skills and on building up her self-esteem and confidence, enabling her gradually to be more involved in social situations, one-on-one or in small group situations. It's about taking small steps and identifying what is most important to her so she can reach her potential and achieve what she wants.

• Be very careful how you say things as they can be taken literally.

• If you take away the reason for developing social interaction and interpersonal relationships, then you can take away the will to try to develop these skills. Emma is not alone in needing a reason to work on things that she finds difficult. In her way of thinking, if there is no reason to do something, there is no purpose and therefore there is no point in doing it.

WORKING /
VOLUNTEERING

Dear Diary,

I thought recently about trying to get back to my volunteering. I felt it was something I should be doing. However, I never quite managed to keep it up. The problem was that my social anxiety severely limits the places that I can spend any length of time in. I wish I could suck it up sometimes, but it's just not possible at the moment. A panic attack involves hyperventilating, crying, feeling all hot and, in my case, rocking, because I also have autism and rocking makes me feel better. So I am not much help to anyone when that happens.

However, sometimes it's a genuine toss-up as to which problem is really the issue when trying to work or volunteer. Sometimes I think it's just the fact I struggle to be around too many people. However, other days the problem has been when someone I am working for does something I feel is wrong. For example, the previously mentioned example my mum gave of when the clothes hangers in the charity shop I volunteered in were hung in a way I considered to be illogical, but which the manager liked. Sure, people will listen to you and make changes sometimes if you explain the issue. They will talk things through. Some people won't. However, nobody can change lots of things about the way they work just because it seems wrong to me.

It's like when my sister and I were walking to the local shop. We both had a certain point where we crossed the road and we both insisted on crossing at our part even though it meant walking separately. However, walking separately was just as bad because I hate being outside the house alone. In some job scenarios in the past, it's felt just like that. I have got jobs but been unable to hold on to them. Partially due to stress and partially due to the fact I just cannot stop thinking about all the tiny little things that bug me. But no matter how much I want to do things my way, the people in charge want to do things their way, and by rights they win.

I am not trying to complain or make excuses. I don't really feel I am, but some people have said that in the past.

You know what job I would really love? I am sure I mentioned this in the entry about shopping, but my ideal job would be sorting shelves. Working for a supermarket, making sure everything is in the right place. Putting back all the things that get put on the wrong shelf or in the wrong section by the customers. Making sure all the shelves are neat, organised and in the right order. I think I would thrive on that. Plus the people contact would be limited because unless people asked me for help I wouldn't really be required to talk to anyone. The occasional one-on-one contact with someone I could probably handle.

Yours,
Emma Louise Bridge

COMMENTARY

Emma has found it hard to maintain any sort of work recently, particularly since we have moved. She has volunteered successfully in the past, although not without stresses, but since our house move she has been unable to do so. As she has said, the two main reasons are the social anxiety and the difficulties with needing things to be a particular way. She does have insight into the fact that she cannot always have it her way, but it is nonetheless stressful for her and has meant she has not been able to continue with volunteering for the time being. That is one reason why writing is a good option for her (as well as her talent) as she can do this from home.

KEY POINTS AND ADVICE

- Look at the underlying problem so you know what to work on.

- Where the social anxiety is due to the number of people, pick carefully what type of work or volunteering you choose and how much face-to-face contact with people there will be.

- Discuss in advance with those in charge any particular needs you may have and how they may accommodate for those needs.

- One difficulty Emma found was turning up and finding the role was different to what she had expected. This is something that needs discussing beforehand to minimise sudden changes or unexpected stressful situations.

- Councils run schemes to help people with a disability gain volunteering or paid employment and will provide support with applications, interviews, on-the-job mentoring and also knowing which employers are more supportive to those with a disability. This will vary from council to council.

- The National Autistic Society also will give advice and support and direct you to local services that are available.

- Life changes such as a house move can result in what seems a 'backward' step, but it doesn't mean that abilities lost cannot be gained again.

- Do not expect too much and always work within the ability levels of the person with ASD/social anxiety. Do not expect great strides forward – small steps are big steps to them.

- Start with short shifts and minimum days, and build up as it becomes possible. Obviously this will have to be arranged with the employer/ manager.

- Try to work with the strengths and talents of the person with ASD

- It is really important that they are not pushed into something that they cannot then maintain. Ultimately, doing so will result in failure and with that they lose confidence and self-esteem.

ROMANCE AND RELATIONSHIPS

Dear Diary,

Relationships make very little sense to me. Honestly, I have had one boyfriend my entire life. We used to meet once a week in town for coffee, which really was an ideal situation for me. I have always dreamed about one day getting married and settling down with a couple of adorable children. However, despite this dream my different view of the world affects my idea of a good relationship, just like it does everything else.

I guess bullet-pointing it would be easiest right now:

- I do not like the idea of someone knowing everything about me. Especially all the really weird bits.

- I don't like change much, so the idea of introducing a new person into my immediate family freaks me out. I managed better with new additions to my extended family. Which is positive.

- I am not sure about having someone I have to care about all the time. Some days I just don't want to hear about people's problems. Some days I just want to know someone is alive and not in pain… I don't know if that is enough for a life partner.

- I don't like physical contact unless I initiate it and it's brief in length. That includes hugs, hand shaking and probably anything more than that. I used to be very huggy when I was little so I am trying to get back to that by hugging my parents. As long as I initiate it, it's going okay.

- I have trust issues. I find it hard to trust people who haven't been in my life a while and proved my affection worthwhile by being a steady presence. I don't mean physically always around but just always in my life. Like my immediate and extended family. If my family already trust them, it makes it easier.

- I find it hard to let things go. When I feel someone has let me down, I find it near impossible to trust them again. The problem is, my rather straightforward, black-and-white, literal world means that people can let me down quite easily. I struggle with making sure I never lose any of my family that way.

- I like everything in my world in a set place and doing things a certain way. It would be hard if someone else wanted to do things a different way.

- I do not really understand the concept of love. I mean, I know I care about my family who have always been around. They are a positive influence in my life and that gives me a good feeling. I don't want to lose any of my family. I just can't picture the idea of that happening with someone new to my life who hasn't previously been a steady and constant person in my life.

However, just because I find things hard to picture or understand does not mean I don't think they could be possible. I still want to find the right guy, settle down and have a couple of children and a dog. I just need a really relaxed partner who goes with the flow, lets me pick everything's place in the house, still just takes on faith that we both care even on days I struggle to show it, knows we both only want each other (relationship-wise) but recognises our need for time alone sometimes, and knows how to recognise a panic attack. Is that too much to ask? Though sometimes my dad finds ignoring me hyperventilating will make me stop. (Depends whether I am panicking for a valid reason or because I feel stressed without remembering why I even started feeling stressed.)

I guess relationships/love is one of those things I don't think I will ever really understand but just have to accept if I want to be happy. There are more things in that category than I can count.

Yours,
Emma Louise Bridge

COMMENTARY

Emma is very honest about her feelings and how she sees relationships, and when she asks or we talk through things, then I am honest with her. We have talked in a previous chapter about the need to build friendships and her wish to not be alone, and I see the way to help her with this is to help her grow in confidence, in her ability in social situations and with her verbal and non-verbal communications skills, to work with her to decrease her social anxiety and so enable her to mix in social situations and therefore meet people and make friends. To help her to become more independent and care for herself and to develop her talents so she is more fulfilled in her life.

It's also important not to expect too much. It is hard that she used to be 'huggy' when young, but we have to accept her for who she is and not expect her to be able to express herself or feel things in a way she cannot. Just because she doesn't show it, it doesn't necessarily mean she doesn't feel it. Also, her tendency to blunt expression can be hurtful and again this is something that we have learned to understand over the years and to accept – although not without challenging her when needed. Through this she has learned to be more guarded in what she says with those outside the family. Not always, though.

KEY POINTS AND ADVICE

- Allow time to listen and talk through feelings, being honest in return about how other people may feel and express themselves or their expectations.

- Either through therapy or family work or both, work on decreasing social anxiety and building up self-esteem and confidence to enter into social situations and meet other people.

- Develop communication skills, both verbal and non-verbal. This can be done in a group setting, as we have done, and also through modelling and demonstrating at home.

- Don't expect too much and don't be offended when affection is not outwardly reciprocated or physical affection has to be instigated one way only.

- Try not to take offence at blunt remarks as they are usually not intended to be offensive.

- Things can change and sometimes for what seems to be the worse, but they can also then change again for the better.

• Remember that other siblings may not understand or react in a positive way to blunt remarks and that misunderstandings can occur. It is important to soothe troubled waters and explain what is meant on both sides.

IT'S JUST A PART OF HOW WE WERE MADE

Dear Diary,

Mum and I had a conversation today about how it's sometimes easy to let having issues be an excuse. I admit I have done that in the past. Said I cannot do this because I have social anxiety. I cannot do that because I have dyslexia. The problem is knowing the line. You do have to know your limitations. Social anxiety is a condition that needs to be taken into consideration. However, you can set your own personal boundaries without using it as an excuse. Especially when you attempt to push those boundaries every day. There are things I have not done because of the social anxiety and some of them I was really sad to miss out on. However, as long as I feel that I made the best decision for me and the people involved, then I think it was a valid choice. When you're not considering anyone else and you just don't want to do something, then you have to think: 'Is this valid? Can I really not do this?'

Autism and social anxiety are closely interlinked. Meltdowns from autism can often be social anxiety/panic attacks. However, I think it's also important that autism and social anxiety should be seen as very different. Social anxiety is a condition that develops and in the same way, with the right work, it can be overcome. Autism is present from birth. You can learn to cope with it and not let it hinder you, but it isn't going to go away. I think that is one of the hardest things to remember but also one of the most important. Autism isn't a disease. You shouldn't think of it as something that prevents you from doing anything. It is something that is a part of you. You don't live your life to the fullest *despite* your autism: you live it *with* your autism. Sometimes when something seems impossible because of the way you think, then you just have to change the approach. Often my mind doesn't understand what other people consider the logical solution to a problem. So instead my mum comes up with an outside-the-box kind of solution. The end result is the same, but the path getting there is different.

Now it's all very well and good to say those things but it's much harder to do it. I struggle and I know I am not the best at sticking with it.

My positive attitude often wavers and I get cross and frustrated. However, I suppose the idea is you keep trying. Keeping focusing on celebrating being different, not being embarrassed by it. I mean, I get that it's annoying. I get that sometimes it feels like 'Why do I get stuck with autism but don't get to have a cool savant gift?' However, being autistic is just a part of how some of us are made.

Yours,
Emma Louise Bridge

COMMENTARY

We have discussed social anxiety and autism and the differences between them. Those who have ASD often struggle with anxiety in social situations which may be caused by many things. One is sensory overload – auditory, visual or tactile. The close proximity of lots of people, lots of noise, lots of visual stimuli, people shaking your hand, wanting to hug you hello, asking questions that you can't answer, having unstructured conversations about things you don't know anything about or don't want to talk about – all these things can be related to ASD. The resultant stress can lead to a meltdown and certain stereotypical self-soothing behaviours that a person with ASD may have developed to cope in such situations. They may also avoid these situations. But social anxiety is a condition separate in itself which can be linked to depression, past experiences, or certain situations which then cause a pattern of behaviour to be repeated, leading either to a panic attack with physical and emotional symptoms or to a refusal to enter into the social situation in the first place. The more stress that is built in the mind, the worse the anxiety becomes and the bigger the perceived threat seems. It is assumed that one's worst fears will come to pass, so it is best to avoid any situation where the perceived threat may arise. Emma tends to find her compulsive traits increase when she is over-anxious.

As Emma has expressed, she believes that the social anxiety will improve and eventually will reduce to a point of not being a problem anymore. As the underlying causes are addressed and she learns to face those situations that she finds so challenging now, she will be able to overcome her feelings of anxiety and participate more fully as she wants to in everyday life.

However, she will still have ongoing challenges related to the ASD which, as she says, is a life-time condition but one that is constantly evolving as challenges are faced and solutions are found to cope with them. I have found being informed, reading, seeking to understand without stereotyping, and looking for the positive and building on our daughters' individual strengths has helped us to help them more. It's important to see ASD in a positive way and build on the positive so they do not see themselves in a negative way and are constantly putting themselves down and struggling with what they cannot do, instead of seeing what they can do. This reflects back to Emma's earlier diary entry about needing praise. When you live in world in which you feel you are different from everyone else and you have struggled and constantly feel people tell you all about the things that are 'wrong' with you, it is hard to see the positive and focus on the good. It is therefore so important to build up their confidence, praise even the smallest things (making sure within families to be aware of siblings and their needs as well) and focus on the positive. A person with ASD may think and feel differently, but they are not 'wrong'; they are just different and unique and have a lot to offer in their own right.

Emma flags up the misconception that all autistic people have a savant gift – a special gift that they excel in. This may be being brilliant at numbers or drawing or some such talent. In our family this has caused upset because it has been seen as unfair to have autism without this savant gift to make it 'worthwhile'. We have also come across this way of thinking from others who have assumed that all autistic people must have a savant gift or that those with high-functioning autism or Asperger's syndrome have minimal issues to deal with. Yes, it is a spectrum and I would not compare anyone, and there will always be those who have greater challenges to face, as with severe autism, but it does not mean – as Emma will tell you and we well know – that those with Asperger's/ASD do not have their share of challenges that can affect their lives in a big way.

KEY POINTS AND ADVICE

- Look at the underlying causes of social anxiety and treat those where possible through a structured programme. Therapy for social anxiety is often very challenging but it can bring the desired results.

- Be informed, read, look on the internet to further your knowledge about ASD and social anxiety. There are many things out there that can help. I have found by reading and understanding more about the conditions that certain behaviours and attitudes, which I had found difficult to understand, now became clear and have enabled me to be more patient and helpful. I have also been able to explain to others when misunderstandings and difficulties have arisen.

- Although it is helpful to be informed, try not to stereotype people as everyone is different, as we know from our girls. Although they may have similarities, they have a host of differences in the way they express themselves, think, feel, perceive and understand – even in the extent to which they wish to inform others of their condition or not and how they feel about it.

- Look at the positive and encourage the person with ASD to see it as part of who they are and celebrate their differences.

- Listen and allow the person with ASD to share, show and help you understand how they think, feel, perceive, etc. They know more about ASD than anyone.

- Don't compare within families.

- Praise and encourage, even for small things.

- Not all people with ASD have a savant gift. This is a misconception.

- As challenges arise, think outside the box to find solutions. Things will change – likes and dislikes, needs, what is tolerated and what is not, obsessions, and so on. It is ongoing.

- Emma has stated she has sometimes used her social anxiety to avoid things that she has not wanted to do. At times I have had to challenge her on this. It has caused arguments, but in the end it has been a learning experience and she has realised is it has been for her benefit to face up to this. It is a sensitive issue and is personal to individuals. I have found I have to not allow her frustrations to upset me when I feel I have to say something; in order for her to progress, she needs at times to be pushed and challenged, even if it is uncomfortable and difficult. This is obviously very personal and different for each person.

ENTRY 78

ALL OR NOTHING

Dear Diary,

I have a set routine because my life works better on routine. This morning I got up at 8:00am exactly. I had a bath which Mum had run for me, did my teeth and brushed my hair. I dressed in my pre-assigned outfit for today. The schedule telling me what clothes to wear is in my special schedule folder. For example, today's clothes are: yellow long-sleeved top, Daisy Duck and Minnie Mouse t-shirt, black and red Betty Boop pants, grey trousers and my Big Bang Theory socks. It does not go well if I forget to do my washing and I often do because my brain seems to think it is something entirely unnecessary to remember no matter how hard I try. Luckily, Mum regularly reminds me because she knows what happens when I don't do it. Though I need to make sure I don't use her as an excuse not to keep trying to remember myself.

The schedule telling me my routine, including the things to do during the day, such as hamster care, is also in my schedule folder. Today my routine also included turning and cleaning my earrings – I had my ears pierced recently – as much as I can manage considering my hypersensitivity makes my pain threshold seriously low. Then I went downstairs and had my bowl of chocolate-flavoured gluten-free star-shaped cereal. I have been told that just listing the day's events is boring. However, I fail to see how explaining my wonderfully perfect routine that allows my life to function properly and keeps the depression at bay could ever be boring. I would totally sit and listen if anyone else wanted to tell me their routine. Though it's likely to be the same as mine because mine works for me so it must work in general.

However, due to the fact I have long-term sleep problems I use my weekend as a free for all. The problem is I can't do just part of my routine. Either I do it all or none of it. So on the weekend I get up when Mum wakes me up because if I am not setting the alarm for 8:00am then I don't set it at all. I don't have my bath unless Mum has run one anyway and calls me to have it. I often don't get dressed and I often don't have breakfast. That's the problem with thriving on a life built on routine. You either stick entirely to your routine or not at all. I find it near impossible to compromise. For example, if I sleep through my alarm for some reason and my waking-up time is ruined on a week day, then often the whole rest of my routine will be out the window and my day will be ruined because my routine is ruined.

Yours,
Emma Louise Bridge

COMMENTARY

Emma thrives on routine and likes structure, as she has described in her diary entry. We have noticed that it very much affects her emotional wellbeing if she is keeping to her well-ordered and laid-out routine or not. It was hard to understand why she did not keep to it at times, as surely all autistic people are obsessed with routine and everything being just so, and will not break their routine for anything! Why could she then apparently stop doing things that she always does? This question shows up how easy it is to stereotype those on the autistic spectrum. We came to realise that there are things that would cause Emma to break the order of her day, but by doing so it caused her stress and affected the rest of the day in a negative way, meaning that none of the routine was followed.

These things could be emotional – depression or low mood, meaning she could not overcome her emotional state enough to complete her routine – and lead to stress and a lowering further of her mood. Practical issues – missing an alarm or not doing her washing so she did not have the right clothes to wear for that day – also lead to stress and an inability to complete the rest of the day's routine because the day had been 'ruined'.

KEY POINTS AND ADVICE

- Unusual changes in routine can be a sign of depression or low mood and need to be monitored carefully, with help and treatment given if necessary.

- Try to ensure that planned washing days and other practical things are in place so that the risk of the routine being disrupted can be reduced.

- Plan with the family so that all needs are taken into account and everyone knows the routine and can accommodate accordingly. It is then important that everyone sticks to their part to ensure the routine is kept, especially when there is more than one sibling on the autistic spectrum.

- It is important for young adults to learn to take responsibility for everyday things, but it is also important to understand and have contingency plans when things go wrong.

- Having more than one of certain items of clothing can help if they are worn a lot.

- Visual reminders and timetables are better than trying to remember. It also helps that the information is there for all the family so everyone knows what is happening and when.

- We encourage some sort of routine at the weekend even if it is not as formal as during the week because Emma does not cope so well with the lack of structure. We encourage her hygiene and dressing routine as part of improving her emotional wellbeing and also her sleep routine.

PUBERTY

Dear Diary,

I don't really remember much about this time in my life. I was only thinking about it today because I found a reminder card for an old doctor's appointment related to blood tests to check my hormones. I remember there was an incident at about the time it started when I stood at the top of the stairs and yelled for Mum that I was bleeding. Mum pelted up the stairs only to find I had knocked a spot and a couple of drops of blood had come out. To me this was a big deal. I was bleeding and it needed to be dealt with. At the time I did not really get that Mum might think something else or even that maybe that wasn't worthy of yelling about. I sort of get it now.

I had issues with puberty but a lot of them weren't related to my autism and aren't really appropriate to write about in my diary. I mean, we aren't supposed to bring it up in conversation so it seems like no self-respecting diary would want to hear about it either. The one big problem that was amplified by my hypersensitivity (see Entry 2) was pain. Whenever I had my time of the month, I would be in pain for the physical reasons I am not describing, but this pain would be amplified further still by just how low my pain threshold is. It got to the point where I was doubled over crying and could barely get out of bed. I know other people have far worse than me, but at the time when it hurt it felt like it couldn't hurt any worse.

The other problem I had was sensitivity to temperature. When I was little, I would be kitted out in boots and a coat every winter just like everyone else. There are pictures of me looking all cute in those over-sized winter coats they sell for children. However, after puberty that changed. Suddenly I didn't feel the cold at all. I would be seen walking around in strappy tops in the snow and Mum had to talk me into taking a coat when we went for walks at Christmas. I never thought it was a big deal, though, as it was kind of nice not feeling the cold. It became a big deal in summer. As I started to really feel the heat, I would feel like I was melting – like in the *Wizard of Oz* when the witch gets water thrown on her – even when other people said it was barely warm.

It got to the point where I would want to hibernate through the summer months and surface again when winter arrived. It also added to the list of reasons why it's really weird I love the beach. Another reason being I burn really easily. I had hormone tests but at the time they could not quite pinpoint the problem. It was only recently that the problem was somewhat solved. I went to have a procedure done to deal with the other issues I have, including the pain. As a result of this procedure the pain is a lot better but also my hormones evened out and my temperature problems got a lot better, showing it was indeed connected to hormones.

Now I still feel the heat but nowhere near to the extent I did. Plus with pale skin and hypersensitivity, a little bit of hibernation in the middle of summer seems reasonable. I also now feel the cold. So much so that I had to go out and hastily acquire a winter coat, long-sleeved pyjamas with proper trouser bottoms, slippers, some jumpers and long-sleeved tops, none of which I had needed before.

The problems I had around this time were not really caused by my autism. However, they were amplified by my hypersensitivity. Plus my difficulties with change meant I struggled with adjusting to the difference before and after puberty. I would leave stuff in the bathroom because I struggled to remember I had to make extra effort to tidy up and throw stuff away now. I didn't put stuff in my bag for emergencies because it was never necessary to do so before. Again, going into details would probably not be great, but I feel it's important to highlight this is a big change in a girl's life and a lot to take in and adjust to. It can seem scary and unfair, and sometimes it was easier to try to push it away and forget about it because it was difficult to adjust. Mum would probably explain it better than me. If you did want to know, Diary.

Yours,
Emma Louise Bridge

COMMENTARY

Emma has described the difficulties she had and the procedure to help with the physical side of her issues related to puberty, periods and hormones. It is important to separate out the medical issues from the hypersensitivity and issues related to the ASD, so that any physical problems can be addressed in the right way and then other issues worked through sensitively and with understanding.

As she writes, Emma struggled with the whole hygiene issue, and I had to gently remind and encourage her in how to manage and care for herself and dispose of sanitary products in a suitable way. This is something that all mothers do with daughters but it took longer with Emma.

We needed to be patient and understanding with the hypersensitivity to pain and blood as she appeared to 'overreact' at what seemed to be the smallest thing.

The change in Emma's sensitivity to cold required gently guiding and adapting and finding suitable clothing that was appropriate for the time of year but still acceptable to her. Emma was resistant to wearing what she saw as superfluous so we had to come to a compromise.

KEY POINTS AND ADVICE

- Distinguish between medical problems which need treatment and those related to ASD which need to be worked through.

- The onset of puberty can cause stress and requires sensitivity and gentle and repeated guidance over a longer period of time than would be normally expected.

- Patience and understanding are needed to deal with what seems to be overreacting to stimuli such as pain, blood, minor injury. Keep calm and reassure.

- When having a procedure in hospital, plan ahead. Ensure the person with ASD knows exactly what to expect, and inform those caring for them of the ASD diagnosis and what issues may arise. Be sensitive to the wishes and needs of the person with ASD and remain calm and patient. We may think how we would react, but they may think and feel differently.

- Have de-stressing techniques if you have to wait for the appointment time or procedure slot. Emma enjoys adult colouring books.

HOSPITALS, DOCTORS AND FEELING ICKY

Dear Diary,

I have been feeling icky over the last few days. The problem is when I feel icky my sleeping problems get worse and so does my anxiety. I have been told everything feels worse when you're tired. Another problem is that I hate things I don't understand and I hate feeling helpless or out of control. Being sick makes me feel both those things. I don't understand a lot of science – I have always been more creative than logical – and I don't really get why my body does a lot of what it does. So when I am sick, I tend not to understand what the doctor's saying when they do tell me what's wrong. I used to take my mum in with me. Recently I stopped because I wanted to feel more grown-up. However, that did not go well at all. I am going to take her in with my every time again from now on. Especially since I don't like to ask the doctor to explain better.

I also feel helpless because being sick messes with my routine. It makes it hard to get up at my usual time. It can affect what I eat – depending on what's wrong – and sometimes I don't want to eat at all. I try to come up with a routine especially for when I am sick, but every bug or virus can affect you differently. I know I can be a bit of a drama queen and Mum is patient with that. However, I get so frustrated and confused. I want to know exactly how long I am going to be ill for, exactly when it will end, exactly what symptoms I will have in what order…and you can't really predict sickness that way.

Luckily, I have not really had anything major. It doesn't help that due to my low pain threshold things become bigger than they are. For example, I had a procedure, mentioned in the previous entry, that usually gets done at the doctor's. However, due to issues, I had to have it done at the hospital under general anaesthetic. This comes with its own problems. Mum came with me and the hospital staff were amazing. However, after I came round from the anaesthetic and my social anxiety kicked in, I started panicking and crying. I couldn't tell them why, though. I was confused by the anaesthetic and in a bit of pain and stressed. I didn't really stop the panic attack until I was safely back with Mum.

Now, again, as I have mentioned before, it's important not to use things as an excuse. I know that. I have to make a note of it again here, though.

I constantly need reminding to try hard to not let being sick get on top of me and mean I give up for a few days. Sometimes being sick calls for retreating to bed. Sometimes you have to try to stick to your routine and struggle on. I am prone to going towards the first one more often than not, but I have promised myself to really try not to. In the same way, I struggle so much with remembering to take my pills. I get cross with Mum when she reminds me because I am really frustrated with myself for having forgotten again, which isn't her fault. I have to work harder on trying to remember.

Being sick can be scary and confusing. It can feel like a big deal even when it's not. It comes with stress and sometimes pain and usually tears. However, my routine will feel all the more awesome when I return to waking up at my usual time without feeling awful, instead of feeling the need to throw up.

Yours,
Emma Louise Bridge

COMMENTARY

Emma highlights several issues which stem from being unwell.

' It messes with her routine.

' It is hard to keep going and easier to settle to the 'sick role' and take to bed.

' By taking to bed, though, her routine is out even more and she feels worse.

' It is important to try to build independence by attending appointments alone, but not feeling able to understand or ask the right questions can mean that the appointment is less helpful than it should be.

' Having a procedure done can cause high levels of stress, leading to a panic attack.

' It can be hard to understand what is going on in your body and it all feels wrong.

KEY POINTS AND ADVICE

' Try to maintain a routine if possible to prevent slipping into the 'sick role' and taking to bed.

' A person with ASD may feel things very differently from others and may feel pain or other symptoms more extremely. This needs to be taken into account and understood and accepted. It is not their fault; it is just the way it is.

• Ensure before any appointment or procedure that you plan ahead, and that those involved know the person has ASD and the issues that may arise from this.

• Judgement is needed when developing independence for the person with ASD and ensuring that doctor's appointments, for example, are helpful and successful. This is a personal decision, but I have found it is important, if you do attend, to try not to speak too much for the person you are attending with. Allow them to take control but give information as and when is needed if they are struggling or do not understand.

• When we informed the staff at the hospital about Emma's ASD diagnosis and discussed prior to the procedure what issues there may be, they accommodated for her needs very well. They treated her like an adult, allowing her to make choices, and were prepared for situations to arise. Although Emma did have a panic attack, they were able to help her until she came back to me.

NOT ALL MELTDOWNS CAN BE 'FIXED'

Dear Diary,

We have just had Christmas and we went to stay with relatives for it. The place we were staying is close to our old house that we haven't sold yet and which I will still consider home at least until we sell it. I thought this might be hard, but actually, with Mum keeping an eye on me, I handled it remarkably well. On the last day we were packing up and from the moment I woke up something felt wrong. I felt stressed and I couldn't work out why. It wasn't until we were getting in the cars that I told Mum something felt wrong, though she had noticed I had been on edge during the morning. I just couldn't pin down what was wrong, though, so I tried to forget about it. For the journey there I had not been stressed, so for the journey home I tried to recreate the same journey. Even though we were taking a different route. I sat in the same seat, in the same car and put on the same music.

It didn't work. I ended up having a meltdown. But there was nothing that could really be done. I couldn't get out the car while it was driving, I couldn't stay behind anyway, and nothing Dad said was getting through to me. In this case I just had to keep crying until I was done. Eventually, I could breathe normally again, I had run out of tears and could talk. It wasn't until then that I managed to work out I was just struggling with the idea of leaving and going back to Cheltenham, because it felt like moving day all over again. I have a hard time expressing myself most of the time, but in this instance I couldn't understand what was wrong myself, let alone explain it to anyone else. Not until I had worked through my emotions did things make sense.

Sometimes panic attacks or meltdowns appear like they are for no reason. I feel like I have no idea why I am feeling stressed or scared. However, I can't think logically and just be okay. Plus deep down there is usually something, a reason. I just haven't figured it out consciously yet. That doesn't make the panic or the stress or the upset feel any less real. I wish all my stressful times could just be talked through and fixed by my family, but sometimes I just need to work it out of my system first.

Yours,
Emma Louise Bridge

COMMENTARY

Sometimes it is hard to pinpoint what is wrong. It can be a feeling that something is wrong and it is not until much later, in the more rational calm after a meltdown, that the reason becomes clear. In this case there was nothing we could do as we had to come home and we had to leave at that time. We were visiting relatives and had to be there by a set time.

De-stressing techniques are individual to each person – although in this case things had just to take their course. When some form of calm returns, it's important to try to work through what caused the problem and why. Our situation is difficult as we are in flux with the move and it is a constant source of stress and tension being in a rented house. When we have sold our old house, this will relieve some of the problem.

By the time we reached our relatives, Emma was calmer, but we allowed her space and time without pressure so she could recover.

KEY POINTS AND ADVICE

- Keep calm and patient.

- Try to pinpoint what is wrong early and avoid the triggers for a 'meltdown'. Even just a feeling that something is wrong indicates a problem.

- Sometimes it is not possible to avoid or prevent a 'meltdown' and occasionally it just has to take its course.

- When calm returns, try to work through what has caused the issues. If it is something preventable for next time or that can be picked up earlier, calming techniques can be used and a meltdown can be avoided. Don't do this too soon as it may cause further distress or panic.

- As we have said before, house moving and all the stresses that go with it, especially when moving into a rented property as an interim measure, can be extra stressful for a person with ASD. This needs to be taken into account and is where keeping routines and as normal as possible is important.

CONCLUSION

I hope this diary is helpful and provides insight and understanding as well as advice. All the advice Mum has given is about moving forward. That is what I hope to do: make little steps forward as often as I can in a move towards one day being independent.

My short-term goals are:

• Trying to work up to being able to get a part-time job so I still have time to write.

• Getting back to the point where I can go to church every week.

• Attending Autismcon, an event in London for those with autism or those helping people with autism.

Then, of course, there are all the things mentioned that I want to keep trying to do – making phone-calls, remembering my pills, not getting angry and frustrated unfairly, etc.

Then I have my long-term goals:

- Writing a novel that is popular and gets turned into a film and then a Lego game.

- Being able to turn writing into a full-time career.

- Working to try to help promote understanding for the causes I believe in – shark welfare, rare-breed protection and understanding autism.

- Getting married and settling down with two adorable children and a dog or two.

I did have going to Disneyland and Harry Potter World on my long-term goal list. I would desperately love to go to both. However, I know that I would struggle with the crowds and the noise.

Finally, my ultimate future goal is:

- To reach the point where my autism is an asset not a hindrance and I live my life to the fullest with my quirks and not despite them.

I would love to have the next 50 years planned out. I like to plan. However, I have had to face that it's best and easiest to take each day at a time and work towards the future in little steps so that I can ultimately make big steps and reach big dreams.

Printed in Great Britain
by Amazon

39118146R00128